PROPEL

Good Stewardship, Greater Generosity

Clayton L. Smith
Foreword by Adam Hamilton

Abingdon Press
Nashville

PROPEL:
GOOD STEWARDSHIP, GREATER GENEROSITY

This book is printed on acid-free paper.

Library of Congress Cataloging-in-Publication Data has been requested.

ISBN: 978-1-63088-368-3

15 16 17 18 19 20 21 22 23 24—10 9 8 7 6 5 4 3 2 1
MANUFACTURED IN THE UNITED STATES OF AMERICA

Contents

Foreword

It is exceedingly important for Christian churches to teach members about their relationship with money. We're bombarded on a daily basis with advertisements seeking to convince us that we'd be happier and more fulfilled if we had newer, better, and more *stuff.* Our economy requires consumer spending, and consumer spending is fueled by the consumer's discontent. The housing market, the manufacturing sector, and the retail industry all require us to become discontent with what we have so that we trade it in for what's new.

Credit cards and consumer loans encourage us to use tomorrow's paychecks to pay for today's pleasures, offering us a lifestyle we cannot really afford. College students are urged to take out student loans for purchases well beyond tuition and books—purchases that may take more than a decade to pay off. Want the car of your dreams? No need to save. Buy it with no money down for seventy-two months. Of course, you'll be upside down in the car for the first three years, but never mind that. All of this borrowing and debt creates stress and negatively impacts our health and relationships.

For those in our congregations who have the means and discipline to avoid debt, there is the lure of "wealth building." We plot out our desirable retirement income level then develop a plan to earn, save, and invest in order to get there. But how much is enough? Will we live to be eighty, ninety, or 100 years old? Will inflation be 2 percent, 3 percent, or 4 percent? What retirement income level will satisfy us? With all that saving and wealth building we come dangerously close to idolizing our investment goals, worshipping mammon instead of God.

There is little room for generosity in a life focused on spending, paying debts, or wealth building. And the charitable giving that *is* done increasingly goes to groups that do an excellent job of asking for money: groups that touch our hearts while helping us feel like we are making a difference. Churches are typically not great at this. In 2013, according to the Giving USA Foundation's "Annual Report on Philanthropy," giving to religious causes declined by 1.6 percent while giving to groups caring for animals and the environment was up 6 percent, giving to the arts and humanities was up 6.3 percent, and giving to education was up 7.4 percent.[1]

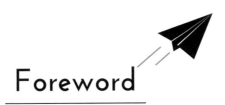

For all of these reasons it is critical that church leaders address the Christian's relationship with money. Jesus said, "One's life isn't determined by one's possessions, even when someone is very wealthy" (Luke 12:15). He said, "Don't worry and say, 'What are we going to eat?' or 'What are we going to drink?' or 'What are we going to wear?'... Desire first and foremost God's kingdom" (Matt 6:31, 33). He said, "You cannot serve God and wealth" (Matt 6:24). He said, "Give, and it will be given to you" (Luke 6:38), and "It is more blessed to give than to receive" (Acts 20:35). Paul commands Timothy to teach the congregation "to do good, to be rich in the good things they do, to be generous, and to share with others. When they do these things, they will save a treasure for themselves that is a good foundation for the future. That way they can take hold of what is truly life" (1 Tim 6:18-19).

The biblical principles of tithing, giving to God, and giving to others can prevent us from becoming enslaved by materialism. When we heed these principles we are less likely to make idols of money and possessions, more likely to honor and glorify God. Indeed our giving is an act of worship, a practice of discipleship, and a way to care for others. It is one way we make possible and participate in God's kingdom work. Our giving is a test of our faith, but it also deepens our faith. Jesus noted that, "Where your treasure is, there your heart will be also" (Matt 6:21).

Stewardship teaching and preaching is not about "pledging the church budget." It is about teaching healthy financial practices. What should a personal budget look like, and why should we use one? What disciplines, tools, and practices can reduce our desire for instant gratification? Why and how should we save for retirement? How do we cultivate a heart of generosity? Of course this approach includes teaching, modeling, and inspiring our congregations to tithe and beyond. It is also pastoral, fostering authentic Christian discipleship, blessing and helping our members. And as people become more generous towards God, churches can do more in mission and ministry.

Clayton Smith has served as Executive Pastor of Generosity at the Church of the Resurrection since 2005. He writes both as one who has earned a doctorate in the field and as one who has spent years as a pastor cultivating generosity in local churches. Clayton has captured important insights and practices in this book. I am grateful for this resource and believe it will help congregation members become effective stewards and joyful, generous givers.

Adam Hamilton
Senior Pastor, Church of the Resurrection
Author of *Enough: Discovering Joy Through Simplicity and Generosity*

Preface

I have the opportunity every year to teach, coach, or consult with several hundred pastors and lay leaders who inquire about how they can improve their financial stewardship and generosity ministry. There is a growing number who want to know how they can improve their leadership skills. Seminary students want to learn what stewardship principles for teaching and preaching today are foundational and will bring lasting results to help their church and members.

This book is my best effort to offer a comprehensive response to the growing interest and need for vital stewardship and generosity ministry. It is designed as a training and planning tool for the finance committee, stewardship and generosity team, endowment committee, memorial committee, strategic mission team, staff, and other leadership teams.

Working on the front line of financial stewardship in the local church offers me an exciting perspective of seeing those who are hungering for a deeper devotion with God through their giving. There are many who want to make a difference now and also want to leave a legacy of love and faith to sustain the future of the church. While not every member is ready to become a generous giver, many are seeking ways to greater commitment. This book is for those who are ready for a transformational challenge. The challenge for our church is to raise the levels of expectation. I believe that good leadership in stewardship ministry will provide the opportunity for greater joy and generosity.

Over the years I have studied in depth theories, theology, and philanthropic philosophies. This is to say that now more than ever before in the history of the church greater attention and leadership is warranted. We sense a great urgency to develop Christian financial leadership in the local church. We search for solid leadership approaches to stewardship and generosity ministry. We strive for more than the latest fad, gimmick, or trending idea.

You are invited to begin a new journey that will propel you to a deeper understanding of financial stewardship and ministry models. Preachers who seek greater understanding about their own personal and family relationships with money will be more effective in preaching stewardship sermons. Preachers who have a deeper passion for the congregational needs, values, and the biblical wisdom for stewardship and generosity will change lives.

For years, many pastors based sermon planning on meeting the budget needs of the local church. This had to change. We now realize that it is not about what the church wants from her members, but what the church wants for her members. We want people to know and experience the joy of generosity in giving to God. People want to be taught how to be better money managers. This new homiletic understanding calls for the dynamic of the preacher's personal concern and urgency for the right use of money. We have learned valuable lessons during economic crisis. Preachers are hearing the call to the teaching task in preaching financial stewardship sermons designed to help people discover financial health, peace, and the joy of generosity. Once this happens, God is glorified and the church grows in giving in ways that can change lives and transform our community.

Each preacher is asked to answer these key questions: How does the preacher's own relationship with money affect the preaching? How is the preacher heard by the congregation? And, does the preacher preach and teach the word of God to produce change so that people can better manage their financial resources, overcome the great burden of debt, and find financial contentment and joy?

The effective financial stewardship sermon will authentically deal with the preacher's personality and pathos, the congregation's context and ethos, and the biblical logos or wisdom. The homiletic model for preaching financial stewardship sermons on the right use of money will help correct our current financial dilemmas and give people hope for the future.

In particular, I, like many of the church leaders, believe that financial commitment is a valid indicator of spiritual health and prognosis. We want to preach the best stewardship sermons possible to bring change, growth, and vision to our congregations that fear decline. Our approach to preaching financial stewardship sermons can move from anxiety to urgency, from feelings of inadequacy to hopefulness. As we teach good stewardship models, great generosity results.

The world of the preacher testifies to the polarity of urgency and ambiguity. Many factors create this tension within the preacher and the church. The Apostle Paul understood its tension when he talked about how grace is not the law and yet it fulfills the promise of the law. In preaching stewardship messages, we encounter both the law and the grace of the gospel. We ask, can God's people give out of joy, duty, or both?

I believe that the preacher's inability to preach an effective stewardship message from the pulpit has created havoc in the church. Signs point in this direction. Many local churches are struggling to survive, and these churches feel little inclination to give money to denominational programs and missions. Furthermore, denominations that formerly had no difficulty funding ministries now face shrinking budgets, staff, and influence. In too many churches the preacher and lay leaders often feel intimidated by pressures to measure our fruitfulness. Preachers motivated by subtle fear, guilt, or even anger, grow empty and frustrated. Fewer people respond and give. Creative and corrective models for all preachers and churches are needed!

We live in a climate of economic stress, uncertainty, incivility in politics, threat of church schism, aging congregations, and donor fatigue in the church. How are we to move forward with sensitivity for donors and a bold vision for Christ and the church? This question calls for an answer. There are so many challenges and opportunities to pastoral and preaching leadership today. The answer lies in raising levels of expectation. I know this from experience.

Each of us can begin to raise our standards and expectations for stewardship and generosity ministry in the local church. While there is a growing awareness and openness about the popular dynamic of generosity in our culture, we still wonder about its impact for the church. In the last few decades, annual giving to religious causes has declined from 52 percent of the charitable dollar to 31 percent while giving to nonprofit organizations has increased every year. Why? I believe the time for asking why is over for those churches that want to do more than survive. New leadership models, focused resources, and improved practices for local church ministry can bring vitality and the joy of generosity.

Our church is like a ship. It turns and changes direction slowly. Our church may have lost its direction as some would say after the 2012 General Conference. Donald Haynes once said about our church: "One thing is sure. If we are to catch the winds that *propel* us forward in voyage, we have to do more than rearrange the deck chairs."[1]

I have been thinking about that prophetic statement for years. I trust that this book on stewardship and generosity can help propel and empower you and your local church forward. Raise your sails. Trust the winds of the Holy Spirit. And know that your preaching and leading skills will be empowered to navigate the troubled waters ahead. I see a new horizon of hope.

Acknowledgments

This little book is dedicated to you, the reader and student of ministry. You are the reason I wrote this book on financial stewardship and generosity—seriously! Now you can say, "I have a book dedicated to me!"

It is written to all who serve Christ and our church and who through generosity can change lives, transform communities, and bring renewal to Christ's church. I am most grateful for the United Methodist churches that I have had the privilege of serving: Schweitzer, Manchester, Centenary, and Resurrection. The leadership of The Church of the Resurrection gave me much encouragement to write. I was also offered a research and writing sabbatical leave that enabled me to prepare this book. I have been blessed by the church over many years.

I do have to say thank-you to all those who lead generous lives for the sake of others!

Let me mention a few by name:

My loving wife and children: Lori, Crista, Caleb, Lindsey, and Blaine

My fantastic assistant at church: Nancy Brown—her support and hard work is amazing

Our Resurrection Executive Team who are partners in ministry: Adam, Sue, Brent, Dan, Debi, Carol, Karen, Glen, Randy, and Amy

Our Resurrection staff who support our Stewardship and Generosity ministry: Kelly, Clif, Cathy, Lee, Kay, Brian, Mary, and many others

All the generous leaders who serve as pastors, bishops, district superintendents, staff, lay leaders, teachers, professors, and consultants in all the churches that I have served

And thanks be to God who called me to ministry on August 15, 1963.

Section I

Leadership, Vision, and Community—Three Essentials

Financial stewardship and generosity ministry is a difficult task for most local church pastors, staff, and elected leaders. Perhaps the greatest challenge facing the church today is to recognize that financial challenges can lead to opportunity. In recent decades we have seen the decline of the mainline church and its impact in our community and world. There is an opportunity for pastors and church leaders today to respond to these challenges and lead, teach, and preach good stewardship practices that result in great generosity!

Seminaries that educate and train our future leaders struggle also with limited financial resources and student enrollment decline. The cost of higher education continues to increase and resources for scholarships for our best theological students decrease. There is an urgent need for better training and resources to grow and sustain our church's future with excellent leaders.

The lack of sufficient funding and good financial stewardship is considered one of the major causes of closing hundreds of churches each year. This section will speak to today's reality but offer help and hope to those leading local churches. In chapter 1 we will discover new ways to hear God's call for excellent leadership. Leadership is the key that will open a future with generosity by addressing the many challenges and opportunities confronting our local churches.

Chapter 2 calls for a new vision for stewardship and generosity ministry. This vision can propel us forward in ways that overcome our fears and decline. Churches today can develop giving resources to help them support and sustain vital ministry and mission through community building and faith development. Chapter 3 will describe the role and practices of the stewardship and generosity team in creating a local church community of generosity. Begin now to think of ways you can enhance your leadership, cast a vision for greater generosity, and build up your community of committed Christians.

Chapter 1

A Call for Leadership

Today, more than ever, focus on the role of leadership in stewardship and generosity ministry matters. Leaders have a sense of urgency in three levels of growing concern:

1. How can we better serve the humanitarian and spiritual needs of all God's people when giving to religion has declined dramatically in the last few decades?
2. How can we better support seminary students, pastors, and religious leaders with leadership skills and financial development tools to create a culture of generosity in the local church?
3. How can we grow and sustain our local churches with essential financial giving in an uncertain economic and conflicted culture?

Our Resurrection Story

Leadership is the key. In 2005, I was appointed to the United Methodist Church of the Resurrection. This appointment was a new executive pastor position created to give specific leadership in the area of generosity. I was to serve on the executive staff. I would focus all of my efforts to develop a comprehensive stewardship ministry and give direction to our church foundation. After serving as a senior pastor for twenty-five years in three local churches, this opportunity for me to specialize was a leadership opportunity and challenge.

My tasks were clearly defined with measurable goals. I joined an outstanding executive team that knew the vital need to grow the financial stewardship ministry. I came to the team after serving as a senior pastor in churches that had a strong record of growing giving and ministry. I had helped establish and develop endowment programs in my three previous churches. I had completed my doctorate studies in the area of preaching financial stewardship. My training and experience seemed like a great match for the needs of the Church of the Resurrection.

In the last ten years at Resurrection we have seen tremendous growth made possible by generous giving. Our operating giving has doubled. Mission giving has more than tripled. We have had three capital campaigns. During the last capital campaign, our congregation pledged $63 million over three years to build our new sanctuary. We now have over five hundred members who plan on leaving a legacy gift to our church foundation to sustain our future ministry, mission, and facility needs. We serve a generous congregation that knows the joy of giving.

Our senior pastor would tell you it is not about him. I would tell you that it is certainly not about me. Yet, I believe the key is leadership. When a local church of any size makes a greater leadership priority out of stewardship and generosity ministry, growth will result. Stewardship leaders can develop clear, measurable annual growth goals as well. I can tell you that having trusted lay or clergy key leaders in stewardship roles will make a difference!

More and more nonprofit organizations are hiring financial development staff. Just investigate your local hospitals, universities, and numerous charities to better understand the growing competition for the charitable dollar. At a meeting in Kansas City, I heard Dave Ramsey appeal to over three hundred church leaders to be sure to staff a paid or volunteer director of stewardship to help people with faith-based financial education. Resurrection has had over twenty-five hundred attend financial education classes with amazing results. It is evident that when our stewardship leaders help our people become better stewards of their financial situation, debt is eliminated, savings grow, and generosity results.

Begin with Leadership

Most church leaders avoid the issues of faith and money because of their personal discomfort or anxiety. And yet, financial stewardship must be given the same visibility and priority as discipleship and other key ministry areas. For too long church leaders have avoided talking about faith and money! For example, until the last five years, most church websites did not list giving and financial education opportunities on the church's home web page.

Every year I consult with more churches that are adding stewardship pastors and staff. There are many new stewardship ministry programs now being developed across our country today that are developing new models for stewardship leadership for the local church. But is it too late? It is not too late for your church if you take action. For example, the Lilly Endowment Theological School Initiative has recently provided grants to several seminaries to examine and strengthen financial stewardship education strategies. These programs will improve the economic well-being and stewardship leadership of future pastoral leaders.

Leadership pays dividends now and in the future. Another vital leadership area that is essential for growth in giving is in staffing (staff or volunteer) for communications and marketing ministry. A congregation that celebrates generosity with excellent and timely information will be a generous church. How can your church improve the way members hear, understand, and respond to giving appeals? Take time to answer this question by using the "Assessment and Audit of Your Stewardship and Generosity Ministry." (See Online Resources.)

Improve Communication

Designing an annual communication plan is also critical. Leadership that articulates the opportunities to change lives motivates givers to offer their best in the coming year. Church members and visitors want to hear what a difference our church has made in the past year. They are excited to learn about new and exciting goals for the coming year. Our people want to know our ministry goals, mission initiatives, and facility and staffing needs. Therefore, a communication plan can provide clear, relevant communication methods that reach all generations and giving levels. Communication can support all areas of ministry, but financial stewardship is a priority.

Expressing gratitude and appreciation for generous giving is the mark of good leadership. This can happen in worship each week as we celebrate the offering as an act of worship. Excellent leaders find creative and effective ways to praise God and also say thank you to those who give. Leaders learn by doing. The more we express appreciation, the better we are at doing it, and donors are blessed.

One of the first priorities of our leadership at Resurrection was to develop and implement a targeted communication model. With the help of staff we identified up to five donor levels of giving for our annual stewardship campaigns. This ministry model helps us speak a relevant message to members at their levels of giving and attendance. For example, there may be up to five different letters written for each mailing. These personal letters express appreciation and invitation, as well as celebrate how our ministry is changing lives, transforming communities, and bringing renewal to the church through generous giving. Carefully worded letters speak to each donor level and encourage increased giving and commitment. Helping donors grow to their giving potential is our goal.

Be Accountable

Leadership works hard to be accountable. Stewardship teams strive to build trust and financial transparency, practice good financial management, and report regularly to leadership and the congregation. They inform our members quarterly of their personal giving records, and enclose an insert that celebrates the ways in which the congregation is changing lives and transforming communities through its generosity. Keeping donors informed of how we make financial decisions is essential. Financial statements and annual audits can be available for review at your finance office. Pastors and staff are prompt to respond to financial inquiries and always express appreciation.

Constantly work on strategic ways to improve the communication of life-changing stories of children, youth, young adults, adults, and those over the age of fifty-five. Strive to identify individuals who have the spiritual gift of giving and are willing to tell their stories. Offer ways in worship and print and social media to make this happen year-round and during our annual stewardship sermon series.

Leaders Create Change

Leadership is responsive and relevant. Too often leadership in the church is slow to respond to the needs of the church and community. This is especially true in the ministry of financial stewardship. In planning operating or capital campaigns, recognize that the theme and sermon series title needs to connect with your congregation. The stewardship focus must call the people of God to change, innovate, and improve.

After the economic recession of 2008–2010, our church launched a capital campaign to reduce our debt. Debt and bad loans were major causes of the recession. Many of our leaders knew that a debt reduction campaign was necessary to the vitality and continued growth of the church. In planning with a professional capital consultant, who had served Resurrection well in all our capital campaigns, we identified several key aspects of leadership that were needed for change.

Leaders Trust God

Know that the journey of generosity will change our lives. This journey begins when we trust God. We give not just because we are expected to support our church. When we trust and then give generously, especially in uncertain economic times, our faith grows stronger.

Before you ask for financial commitment, ask your leaders and members to begin a prayerful discernment process to first truly trust God. Engage people in a prayer process that is the foundation for their thoughtful decision-making process. In other words, our journey of faith leads us to trust God more than out of a sense of duty to give to a budget or specific ministry initiative.

Leadership that is based on trusting God believes that the best is yet to be. "Instead, desire first and foremost God's kingdom and God's righteousness, and all these things will be given to you as well" (Matt 6:33).

Leaders Communicate Compelling Vision

I have witnessed that one of the most powerful outcomes of effective stewardship campaigns is the deep conviction that the campaign connects to the vision and purpose of the church. Spiritual growth results with deeper commitment to Christ and the church. The vision and purpose become foundational to every financial campaign.

Every member is invited to be on the same page at the same time to move together to the future. A clear and concise communication plan needs to speak to the non- and nominal Christians as well as to the most faithful and generous givers. This campaign vision and case statement will be able to speak to each donor level according to its need and potential. The leader's task is to communicate the compelling need and vision.

Your Leadership Example

Leaders give and their giving sets the pace for others. As a leader, you represent the standard of excellence that is needed in generosity. Leaders communicate their personal example of tithing as they share their faith and giving story. In capital campaigns, leaders lead by giving sacrificially above the tithe. While others may not reach the standard you set, members will be highly motivated to do their best.

Paul reminds us, "They gave themselves to the Lord first and to us, consistent with God's will" (2 Cor 8:5).

Your personal leadership to discern God's will for yourself and your church will energize the congregation. Your example of financial commitment will set the pace, and your recruitment and involvement of other key leaders who are generous givers will make the difference.

Leaders Stay Positive

Today's culture demonstrates many signs of uncertain and conflicted American lifestyles and values. At Resurrection, as with any church, we find people experiencing what we call "donor fatigue," lamenting, "Another financial campaign!" There are also many other issues that are lying just below the surface, especially when we talk about faith and money.

Leadership always listens. After listening, leaders can communicate these issues and needs in a way that will accentuate the positive. At the same time, leaders can draw out the problems to better handle the challenges facing the church. Most challenges, when addressed faithfully, can become opportunities.

The leader's objective response to these issues is critical to the success of creating leadership trust and a climate of generosity. Members are reminded of what Jesus said in Matthew 6:21, as Christ talked about the most important priority: "Where your treasure is, there your heart will be also." We lead for the sake of Christ above all. Caring enough to deal with conflict in a positive way brings personal and spiritual growth.

Leaders Express Sincere Appreciation

Another key leadership quality for generosity to flourish is found when leaders take the time to humbly say "thank you" to all levels of donors. This is done in worship where the dynamic of gratitude is celebration. Expressing appreciation can be done personally through phone calls, e-mails, and correspondence. Send thank-you notes to first-time donors. Saying thank you can never be done too much! Leaders communicate appreciation with clarity. There is power in gratitude! In my ministry I have discovered great joy in expressing thanks!

Develop a Team Spirit

Leadership trust in the church is the glue that holds the staff and church governance together. Building teamwork is based on consistency of the message, loyalty, and support of each other. There is also a need for delegation of authority, an activity schedule, constant accountability of each team member, and constant affirmation of all involved. Taking risks is rewarded in leadership, and mistakes are not recognized as failures. Even good leaders make mistakes and then are quick to take responsibility. Proverbs 24:16 says, "The righteous may fall seven times but still get up, but the wicked will stumble into trouble."

Team spirit and execution are especially critical components of stewardship programs. Celebrate the team's work!

Leaders Transform Challenges into Opportunities

Many churches have gone through the last few years of economic uncertainty. Adam Hamilton spoke to church leaders that there "is a blessing behind economic uncertainty for the church." Adam's preaching and teaching compelled our members to stop living above their means, to get out of debt, and to put God first in their efforts to reset priorities.[1] His sermon series invited members to a life of simplicity, generosity, and joy. Our fears were transformed by faith and deeper trust. Adam's book, *Enough*, also tells a powerful story of how our church responded to the challenge of the economic recession.[2]

Leaders Understand Past Challenges

If our church is to have a future we will need to know our financial challenges and respond with intentional leadership. Lovett Weems makes an observation about the United Methodist Church: "For thirty years through 2007, United Methodist congregational giving as a whole, which means all giving for all purposes by all churches, increased $100 million to over $300 million annually before factoring in inflation. That stopped in 2008 when the gain was less than $5 million, as the national recession made its impact. Then in 2009, there was an absolute decline of almost $60 million."[3]

The dilemma facing most mainline churches is seen in the decline of membership, attendance, and giving. Also, our churches are aging at an alarming rate! As has been noted already, giving to religion in the United States has declined from 52 percent of all charitable donations to 31 percent in the last fifty years. Giving to religion continues to decline as reported in the Report of Giving USA: Annual Giving Report on Philanthropy.[4]

The 2007–2008 great recession and stock market crash had both a positive and negative impact on giving to religion. There are many churches, including Resurrection, that saw cautious growth in giving during this period of financial uncertainty.

Those congregations that did well had a strong history of good stewardship ministry models. These churches started programs for financial coaching, budget, and debt reduction. Church members were challenged by preaching and teaching to stop living above their means, start saving, and remember the needs of charity.

Congregations that did poorly were those who were hit hard due to unemployment, geography-related economic issues, and not making financial stewardship teaching ministry an essential part of worship and education.

One writer indicated that the economic recession demonstrated the survival of the fittest in religious communities. The challenge for the church today and tomorrow is to develop sustainable financial resources by greater emphasis on financial stewardship and generosity. For this to happen there needs to be a paradigm shift: *It is not what the church wants from our members but what the church wants for our members.*

Leaders Comprehend Cultural Challenges

Cultural changes continue to negatively impact the religious culture and bring decline to the church. This is most evident in measuring charitable giving. Giving USA reported that between 1966 and 2012, religious giving dropped 20 percent.[5] At the same time we have seen increased giving to nonprofit organizations in the last several decades. The decline of the mainline church attendance and the mission impact in the local community has also had a significant impact on giving.

One of the most difficult observations for the church is that while local church budgets may have increased, the percentage amount of funding for mission and benevolence has shrunk. Of course, there are exceptions to this observation. Many other local churches and denominations are seeing growth in giving especially to aid emergency and disaster causes. We are seeing more attention to literature and training programs designed to improve local church giving. Good stewardship leadership practices are making a difference.

Today's culture has seen a significant rise in media attention to generosity and philanthropy inside and outside of faith communities. Across the American culture we can celebrate growth in humanitarian giving. We can also lament limited giving for religious giving. This giving decrease will continue to impact the church and our needy world for decades to come unless we can reverse this trend of giving less to religion.

In spite of the decline of religious giving in our society and the economic recession, there is good news about the generous nature of religious people. People of faith are still more generous than the non- or nominally religious. In 2000, religious families gave three and a half times more money to charity than secular people whose incomes were similar.[6] This fact is valid today and yet we have observed a significant decline in membership in the church.

Most people report that their giving grew out of their faith experience. High expectation churches that teach tithing and percentage giving see greater generosity because of their clear expectations. Arthur Brooks says, "The main reason most religious people give is out of a 'sense of duty.'"[7] However, in recent years I have observed a decline in this priority as loyalty to the church wanes.

Studies also indicate that religious affiliation does make a significant difference in giving. Those churches that teach high giving expectations receive greater donor generosity. There are other motivations today for generosity besides "sense of duty" that will be addressed later.

Leaders Recognize Generational and Gender Opportunities

Another dynamic challenge in our culture is seen today in the way younger generations give. This is reshaping the landscape of generosity. More than ever, age matters in giving! The boomer generation is less generous than their pre-war parents. And the end of life-cycle giving potential for religious giving is greater for religious contributions than secular.[8] The church now has a responsibility to ask for bequests and other planned gifts if our future is to be sustained.

Our consumer culture also means that more expendable income available in our society does not mean greater charity. This is true for all age groups, especially those over the age of fifty. For example, the boomer generation is the most unchurched generation today with the greatest potential for generosity for tomorrow. At the Church of the Resurrection, we have launched a new Crossroads ministry to help this generation navigate the second half of their lives. We discovered that the number of boomers in our church has increased by 400 percent in the last ten years. We have offered well-attended pre-retirement seminars the last three years for this age group. The number one concern voiced at these seminars for the boomers has been in the area of financial planning and security for retirement. Boomers also want to leave a legacy that can change lives and sustain a vital future for our church. This new ministry is also sponsoring workshops on social security, Medicare, and estate and legacy planning. Workshops especially designed by and for women around financial planning are also popular. All these workshops help our visitors and members recognize that good stewardship offers greater generosity opportunities.

There is also a growing awareness about the primary role women play today in philanthropy and giving. For example, single women are more generous than single men. The fact that more women are single today adds to this impact. Women also live longer than men and make the most legacy gifts. Gender matters in giving! The challenge for the church is to develop programs to help women with stewardship and generosity teaching so that they can reach their giving goals, while providing for themselves the necessary financial income to live a quality and financially secure life.

Leaders Measure and Benchmark Capacity

A key question for each church is: "How do you analyze your church's overall annual commitment and capacity for giving?" It may be helpful to do a stewardship and generosity audit in order to measure the last three years of total giving. What trends do you see? What are your giving strengths? What are the weaknesses? What are the opportunities to improve? And what threats to your giving do you anticipate? This SWOT Analysis is essential and can be completed every three to five years as you update your strategic stewardship plan. (See Online Resource: "Assessment and Audit of Your Stewardship and Generosity Ministry.")

Nonprofit Challenge to the Local Church

A major challenge facing the church is the growth of nonprofit charities. These organizations do much good in our communities, but the competition for the charitable dollar is fierce. Lyle Schaller puts it this way: "This new face of American philanthropy is distinguished by an unprecedented level of competition for the charitable dollar. For well over 90 percent of all Christian congregations . . . this means they will not be able to compete . . ."[9]

How can the local church compete with universities, hospitals, and hundreds of worthy nonprofits when many of them have over ten, twenty, or even a hundred full-time fund-raising staff? Most churches have volunteers or part-time staffing for fund-raising needs. The lack of trained leadership will be a growing challenge for the church.

How then can we preach and teach "certain faith in uncertain times" in a financially competitive culture? This task is challenging but essential in turning fear into deeper faith and trust. Many churches are struggling to simply maintain their ministry budgets and increase giving to mission. There has been a seismic shift in donor attitudes. Giving will remain low and limited unless we address this challenge directly. How can leaders develop a fresh donor-based teaching approach to grow the needs of a congregation's personal confidence in giving? Let's begin by identifying some of the church's growing competition for the charitable dollar.

Leaders Honor Their Donors

How do we clearly communicate the financial stewardship message when our members are already overloaded with an avalanche of requests for giving? We get as many requests in a week compared to what our parents previously got in a year. Add daily e-mail and web-based marketing requests for giving and we all feel overwhelmed. Donors are fatigued by so many requests.

How can the church better minister to the financial fears of our members? We can provide support to our members. This is the most important pastoral role of the church! The pastoral challenge is how to best relate to the donor's fears and needs.

People long to hear ways to improve their financial situation. Here are the top five financial fears facing all of us:

1. Fear of losing our financial security
2. Fear of outliving our income, savings, and social security
3. Fear of escalating medical costs
4. Fear of increasing tax burden
5. Fear of not being able to support church and charity needs

Leadership that addresses these fears through relevant preaching and teaching will help people grow in faith through economic and personal financial uncertainty. How do we bring the dilemma of the church's needs and the donor's fears together in a way that best serves God's greater good? We can address these challenges in creative new ways. We can and must help our members become better stewards of their financial resources so that they can become generous givers.

The Pastoral Care Challenge

We need clear expectations about excellent care by pastors and congregational care lay ministers. The following ten suggestions can help improve your pastoral care challenges with opportunities for new ministry:

1. Develop new ministry and mission opportunities that attract and involve those over the age of fifty.
2. Assist members as they seek ways to give financially at any level. Help them find the joy of generosity.
3. Offer encouragement, financial coaching, and other learning opportunities to those needing help with personal financial management.
4. Invite members and others to share their stories of giving that changed lives.
5. Provide pastoral care to those going through personal loss or financial difficulty. In most cases, exclude them from any financial appeals of the church during this time.
6. Be sure to practice confidentiality at all times. Some members prefer to give anonymously and appreciate opportunities to give to needs of the church. Nurture those relationships.
7. Encourage members to plan legacy gifts with the help of the church's planned giving ministry. Help donors fulfill their dreams.

8. Inform members of the ways in which memorial gifts can honor their loved ones and provide vital needs for the church's ministry and mission.
9. Be sensitive, caring, and considerate of those seeking ways to make a difference through generosity and joy. This is especially true for nurturing major donors.
10. Develop a three-year plan to add staff and volunteers to enhance your new stewardship and generosity ministry. This strategic planning is the first step, not the last, in meeting pastoral challenges for the church today and tomorrow.

Now, more than ever before, expertise in financial stewardship ministry is needed. Stewardship and generosity ministry must become a greater priority in the local church. Volunteer and staff leadership can be developed. The joy of giving can be contagious for growth in ministry and mission. Excellence in pastoral care can nurture the culture of generosity year after year.

Denominational Challenges Impact Leadership

For example, the aftermath of the 2012 General Conference of the United Methodist Church added up to many disappointments and delusions about institutional reform. Many denominations have an increased level of distrust in leadership because of a failure to streamline structure; and as a result, our leaders have a greater level of distress. Also, there is a constant threat of denomination schism over issues of theology and sexuality.

This denominational challenge is compounded by our continued economic uncertainty and decline in membership. We hear the lament "doing more with less" becoming "doing less with less." At the same time there is greater missional need for the poor, increased costs of health care, and reduction of future pension support. We have an aging denomination and younger generations less likely to support institutional giving. Denomination leaders are seeking new ways to increase generosity at all levels of the church. One of the positive changes in the 2012 Book of Discipline was adding the chairperson of the local church stewardship team to the finance team. "Amid some of these worrisome trends, we continue to have strong signs of life in our churches," says Scott Brewer of the General Council of Finance and Administration.[10] Contributions rose by 146 percent in 2010 and 2009, in part due to contributions to Haiti for earthquake relief. Yes, the mission giving of our churches continues to grow!

One observation that this writer would make has to do with the wonderful way congregations give to emergency appeals. No one hesitates to ask for money when a disaster happens. As a matter of fact, everyone asks. When people know and understand the need, they respond generously. It should not take an emergency to motivate leaders to ask people to give generously. And yet, when leaders call the church to action we are motivated to be our best and nurture unity in a diversity of challenges.

Leaders Take Action

Research tells us that there are several key factors for increased giving in your active membership. First, those who practice regular prayer, Bible study, worship, and serving give more. Second, those connected to a small group, class, or project team will give more. Third, when the church's vision and purpose are communicated each year to support generosity, giving increases. Fourth, celebrate the many ways that generous giving is fulfilling the church's mission and purpose. Fifth, look for new ways to reach different age levels of your congregation. (See Online Resource: "Crossroads: Navigating the Second Half of Life—Strategic Plan.")

There is good news for those who realistically face these and other challenges to then discover great opportunities. The wealth, generosity, and charity of the baby boomer generation in our society are having an unprecedented impact on mission needs, both locally and internationally. For the first time in history the older adult population controls more than three-fourths of America's wealth.[11] With this boomer generation comes an unparalleled opportunity. Many are asking about legacy gifts. Church leaders can offer timely workshops on estate planning and encourage legacy gifts to help sustain our future ministry and mission. Church leaders can also offer estate and financial planning seminars designed especially by and for women. The time for action is now.

Leaders Seek Training

Bill Hybels said at the 2013 Willow Creek Global Leadership Summit, "When a leader gets better, everyone wins." It is observed that 95 percent of leaders say that leadership development is crucial to their staff; and yet, only 25 percent are taking action toward their leadership development. One of the best training experiences our stewardship leaders received was a two-year program provided by the Leadership Network for Generous Churches. The Horizons Academy of Faith and Money also offers an exciting intensive and comprehensive training program.

There are a number of ways local churches can become generous churches. Churches can begin to do leadership training for financial stewardship. Pastors will discover a deeper understanding of what the Bible says about money and generosity. New leadership tools, igniting trends, and best practices are readily available each year and can be found at www.cor.org/tools. For example, every year Resurrection hosts a Leadership Institute. Financial workshops are offered to teach relevant information on generosity, annual stewardship campaign planning, capital campaigns, and planned giving programs. More training opportunities will be available as the growing need for good stewardship training is evident.

The Power of Leadership

Now, more than ever, leadership counts in the area of financial stewardship. Leaders connect the mission statement of the church to the purpose of giving. Leaders celebrate giving that brings vitality and generosity. Leaders teach that giving is an act of worship that fulfills the church's primary ministry and mission. Leadership training is essential each year to learn the current trends of giving. Leaders communicate with clarity of purpose.

It is all about leadership. Your leadership can influence, inspire, and instruct people to reach the common good and purpose of the church community through generosity.

Online Resources

Assessment and Audit of Your Stewardship and Generosity Ministry

Crossroads: Navigating the Second Half of Your Life—Strategic Plan

Chapter 2

Casting a Vision for Stewardship and Generosity

I have loved to fish ever since I caught a big bass at my grandfather's lake when I was five. Since that day I feel the excitement and challenge of fishing as I dream of catching the biggest fish ever. I am a student of the sport of fishing. Bernard "Lefty" Kreh is a top fishing instructor if you want to learn the "art" of fly casting. I study Lefty's DVD instructional teaching tips, which are the best. A good fisherman studies the fishing habitat and knows what the fish are attracted to during different seasons and weather. The art of casting is effectively putting the lure where the fish are. Casting the vision to meet the needs of his people is what Jesus did. He went to the seashore and called his disciples to be fishers of men. He cast the vision of the kingdom of God for all people.

Adam Hamilton is among the best pastors in the country, especially if you want to learn the "art" of vision casting. Over the years I have helped a number of churches develop their vision and mission statements. But I never have seen a church be so focused and driven by their vision as I experience it at the Church of the Resurrection. We are a vision-driven church! We have a clear and compelling purpose. Every day we make decisions that help fulfill our vision and purpose. Nearly every week Adam reminds us of our vision and purpose in worship, meetings, and staff events. These statements offer clear, compelling, and concise direction:

> Resurrection's Vision: ***Changing lives, transforming communities, and renewing the church.***
>
> Resurrection's Purpose: ***To build a Christian community where nonreligious and nominally religious people are becoming deeply committed Christians.***

Vision and Purpose

The culture of generosity is based on vision. People give to change lives, transform community through mission, and bring renewal to churches. To generate support for generosity be sure to constantly communicate the church's purpose and vision. Every member is expected to be able to recall and communicate the church's purpose. Also, visitors will respond with enthusiasm when asked to support the purpose of the church if they are informed and invited to do so on a regular basis. Everyone wants to be part of a compelling vision and purpose! It becomes the invitation to involvement as every week we seek to know, love, and serve God.

The vision and purpose of the church can be integrated in every area of ministry. Vision empowers our financial stewardship ministry. Every stewardship campaign, stewardship class, or planned giving seminar can support the purpose and vision of the church. Communication of this vital relationship of giving to support our church's vision and purpose becomes a core value of every member's spiritual growth.

Courage and Conviction

At the 2013 Willow Creek Global Leadership Summit, Bill Hybels proclaimed that vision was the most important tool a leader can use. He confessed that in his leadership role it took great courage to move people from what is to what could be. Having courage is essential to making vision a reality. Pastor Hybels invoked this scripture from Joshua 1:9: "I've commanded you to be brave and strong, haven't I? Don't be alarmed or terrified, because the Lord your God is with you wherever you go." Bill Hybels reminded us that vision is the most potent weapon in the hands of a leader!

Having vision is one thing. Having the courage to do something with it is another. This is especially true when God calls us to step out in faith to launch a financial campaign. Fear around fund-raising causes many leaders to become paralyzed. They cannot move forward. They are frozen in their fear; and yet, vital leadership can and must overcome these fears with faith that makes vision a reality.

Leadership trusts in God for the vision to change people. Leadership also has the courage to define the current reality and needs for the future of the church. Most churches can be evaluated in one of three ways: decline, status quo, or growth. When leaders compare God's vision to the current reality, they recognize that in decline and status quo situations, there must be urgency for action and change. Having vision and courage is a gift of certain faith in uncertain times.

At Resurrection, the vitality of our dynamic vision and clear and compelling purpose continues to direct all that we do. In our stewardship ministry, we communicate the following complementary purpose statement:

To build a Christian community where nonreligious and nominally religious people are becoming deeply committed Christians that demonstrate good stewardship and the joy of generosity.

Good Stewardship Propels Great Generosity

My bishop, Robert Schnase, tells this story on me in his devotional book on practicing generosity:

> A few years ago, I had the privilege of speaking at a training seminar at a large United Methodist church. My host was on staff at the church, and he described how he had recently changed his title after reflecting upon the book *Five Practices of Fruitful Congregations* (one of the five practices being "extravagant generosity"). Formerly the Executive Pastor of Stewardship, he was now the Executive Pastor of Generosity. He, the other staff, and the congregational leaders decided "generosity" comes closer than "stewardship" to describing his purpose and role.
>
> This made me think. What's the difference between "stewardship" and "generosity"? What comes to mind when you hear those words? For what distinctive purposes are they best suited? How do people respond to those terms?[1]

In over forty years of ministry, I have observed that the word *stewardship* has lost its impact. We know that a steward is someone who manages the owner's property. Comprehensive stewardship is good management of our time, talents, service, environment, relationships, and so forth. Financial stewardship becomes lost in the long list of understandings and needs. We need greater clarity and focus on financial stewardship and generosity today.

In his book *Money, Possessions, and Eternity*, Randy Alcorn agrees that the word *stewardship* has fallen on hard times but then concludes, "It is such a good word both biblically and historically, that it deserves resuscitation rather than burial."[2] Gordon MacDonald echoes his support with the observation that stewardship is among the Bible's greatest and most significant themes.[3]

Ron Blue describes stewardship from a biblical sense as the use of God-given gifts and resources (time, talent, treasure, truth, and relationships) for the accomplishment of God-given goals and objectives.[4] Blue explained that stewardship means making wise decisions about how you use your time, talent, and money, whereas generosity is the willingness to give or share what you have for the benefits of others.[5] When we add the word *generosity* with *stewardship*, our focus on financial giving has clarity and empowerment.

As executive pastor of generosity, I always try to be a good example of the word *generosity*. Having been blessed with generous parents, pastors, and other role models, I have always enjoyed giving. We all know God loves a joyful giver (2 Cor 9:7). Bishop Schnase goes on to describe generosity:

> Generosity is an aspect of character. It is an attractive quality which I aspire to and desire to see cultivated in my children. The opposite of generosity is selfishness, self-centeredness, greed, and self-absorption. Generosity extends beyond just the use of money, although it most definitely includes that. There are generous spirits; generous souls; people who are generous with their time, with their teaching, with their love. Generosity finds many biblical sources, and is a fruit of the Spirit (Galatians 5:22-23). It sounds more organic, more generative, less legalistic, less formal than stewardship. I have to explain to my teenage sons what stewardship means. They know generosity when they see it.[6]

Like most pastors, I have served churches full of generous people. I confess that I have failed to celebrate generosity as an act of worship. Many local church pastors and worship leaders fail to celebrate generosity in worship and miss out on the opportunity to express the joy of generosity. I believe generosity needs to be celebrated and encouraged. Churches need someone (staff or volunteer) to constantly remind the members of the church's vision of stewardship and generosity. Your stewardship and generosity team can fulfill this vision and give leadership for financial ministries designed to help others be better money managers and generous givers. Every time we celebrate large and small gifts we help proclaim the vision of generosity as a witness of faith.

Bishop Robert Schnase identifies the personal and spiritual benefits of generosity:

> Generosity focuses on the spiritual qualities of the giver, derived from the generosity of God, rather than on the church's need for money. One of these terms is not superior to the other. Perhaps there are shades of difference in how they are perceived by young and old, those new to the faith from those long-established in our churches. Maybe using both wisely helps us reach people at different places on the journey of faith. Whatever term you use, the bottom line is that churches must emphasize the Christian's need to give more than the church's need for money.[7]

I encourage every local church to use the terms *stewardship* and *generosity*. If you teach and preach good stewardship, great generosity will result. Helping people become better money managers gives them the opportunity to practice the joy of generosity. We can observe those who discover their spiritual need to give as an act of worship. They celebrate generosity and experience dynamic doxology!

These two ideas—stewardship and generosity—are best seen together, as MacDonald reminds us:

> Generous living is more often a measure of one's soul than of one's pocketbook. . . . People who live generously share a firm conviction that a generous portion (that's the generosity part) of what they have must be strategically given (that's the stewardship part) for the betterment of others and for the advancement of God's kingdom. . . . Stewardship is at the heart of the discipline of generous giving. With-

out it, giving becomes a miserable experience, and truly generous giving may not even be possible.[8]

Expanding the Principles and Practices of Wesley

The first time I Googled the word *generosity*, I discovered the quote from Rev. John Wesley, eighteenth-century revival leader and founder of the Methodist movement. In Wesley's sermon "The Right Use of Money," he identifies a three-point vision/purpose for stewardship and generosity:

1. **Gain (earn) all you can** (without hurting yourself or your neighbor).
2. **Save all you can** (save all you can by cutting off every expense that serves only to indulge foolish desire; waste nothing).
3. **Give all you can** (do not limit yourself to this or that proportion... a tenth... a third... a half. Give all you can to God... that you may give a good account of your stewardship).

Wesley had a clear vision for the church of his day. While preparing for a Wesley Heritage Tour, I discovered that John Wesley was very effective in capital campaigns for the New Room in Bristol and especially for the Wesley Chapel in London. His vision spoke revival and generosity! He communicated clearly the joy of salvation that resulted in generous living. John Wesley's message spoke to the needs of revival England in the eighteenth century. His sermon "The Almost Christian" alienated the sophisticated Oxford community. His sermon on the use of money (February 17, 1744) was based on the parable of the dishonest manager (Luke 16). Wesley concluded with this appeal: So "laying up for yourself a good foundation against the time to come, that you may attain eternal life!"

In Wesley's day there was a great gap between the rich and the poor. We have that growing gap today and Wesley's message can be even more relevant. Today, too many members of our churches live above their means, save little, are slaves to debt, have a lack of honesty about their financial struggle, and therefore, give little. How can our church help people find financial freedom from the slavery of debt?

The church's teaching is more than to simply earn more, save more, and give more. Our task is to get at the heart of the matter for the benefit of those we serve. We are called today to teach stewardship in order that people will be better money managers and eventually experience the joy of generosity. The church can teach biblical truths that reveal transformation from the self-centered to God-centered life. I believe that good stewardship and sanctification go together and represent God's vision for the people of God.

Wise stewardship flows out of a life devoted to God. The transformation of the heart brings sanctification to our living and giving. In my ministry with generous givers, I observe the ways in which spiritual and material values are woven together. The joy of good stewardship and generosity will be a mere reflection of the glory of God when we hear, "Well done, good and faithful servant" (Matt 25:21, 23 ESV).

Wesley's Expectations

When we study John Wesley's stewardship-based message to earn, save, and give all you can, we find biblical support and deeper understanding. Wesley based his expectations on the biblical story. The following scriptures inform our understanding of stewardship:

First, how and why do we *earn all we can*?

> The LORD God took the human and settled him in the garden of Eden to farm it and to take care of it. (Gen 2:15)
>
> There are different spiritual gifts but the same Spirit; and there are different ministries and the same Lord; and there are different activities but the same God who produces all of them in everyone. A demonstration of the Spirit is given to each person for the common good. (1 Cor. 12:4-7)
>
> The lazy don't roast their prey, but hard workers receive precious riches. (Prov 12:27)
>
> Whatever you do, do it from the heart for the Lord and not for people. You know that you will receive an inheritance as a reward. You serve the Lord Christ. (Col 3:23-24)

Second, how does God teach us to be prudent and *save*?

> Thus says the LORD, your Redeemer, the Holy One of Israel: I am the LORD your God, who teaches you for your own good, who leads you in the way you should go. O that you had paid attention to my commandments! Then your prosperity would have been like a river, and your success like the waves of the sea. (Isa 48:17-18 NRSV)
>
> Reliable people will have abundant blessings, but those with get-rich-quick schemes won't go unpunished. . . . The stingy try to get rich fast, unaware that loss will come to them. (Prov 28:20, 22)
>
> Tell people who are rich at this time not to become egotistical and not to place their hope on their finances, which are uncertain. Instead, they need to hope in God, who richly provides everything for our enjoyment. Tell them to do good, to be rich in the good things they do, to be generous, and to share with others. When they do

> these things, they will save a treasure for themselves that is a good foundation for the future. That way they can take hold of what is truly life. (1 Tim 6:17-19)

Third, how does God want us to *give all we can*?

> Give, and it will be given to you. A good portion—packed down, firmly shaken, and overflowing—will fall into your lap. The portion you give will determine the portion you receive in return. (Luke 6:38)

> In everything I have shown you that, by working hard, we must help the weak. In this way we remember the Lord Jesus' words: 'It is more blessed to give than to receive.' (Acts 20:35)

> Where your treasure is, there your heart will be also. (Matt 6:21)

> What I mean is this: the one who sows a small number of seeds will also reap a small crop, and the one who sows a generous amount of seeds will also reap a generous crop.
>
> Everyone should give whatever they have decided in their heart. They shouldn't give with hesitation or because of pressure. God loves a cheerful giver. God has the power to provide you with more than enough of every kind of grace. That way, you will have everything you need always and in everything to provide more than enough for every kind of good work. As it is written, He scattered everywhere; he gave to the needy; his righteousness remains forever.
>
> The one who supplies seed for planting and bread for eating will supply and multiply your seed and will increase your crop, which is righteousness. You will be made rich in every way so that you can be generous in every way. Such generosity produces thanksgiving to God through us. (2 Cor 9:6-11)

Paul encouraged generosity at all times: "While they were being tested by many problems, their extra amount of happiness and their extreme poverty resulted in a surplus of rich generosity" (2 Cor 8:2). It is important to teach that good stewardship is serving God by managing all that God gives us. Stewardship is not just the means for our church to raise money to support ministry. Good stewardship is a way of life that benefits everyone as we recognize that everything we have is a gift from God. As Christians we are called to be good managers for the benefit of ourselves, our family, and our church family while we are here on earth. Teaching good stewardship empowers great generosity.

The Bible is filled with hundreds of examples of grateful response to God's generous gifts. By devoting over two thousand verses to the topic of material possessions, the Bible teaches that each of us has a personal responsibility to share with others and warns against selfishness and misuse of God's financial resources.

There are many passages on money and wealth that tell us the purpose of stewardship is not what God wants from us but what God wants for us. "What are human beings, that you exalt them, that you take note of them, visit them each morning, test them every moment?" (Job 7:17-18). God wants to encourage us to be rich toward the Lord. As we become more like Christ, our hearts are transformed and we become conformed to the image of Christ. We can become generous, just as God is generous. The nature of God is to be generous.

Local Church Expectations

Setting clear expectations is essential. Reminding members of these expectations on a regular basis is a priority for growth in faith and in giving. At Resurrection we emphasize that giving is an act of worship. Our giving makes possible the vision of our church to change lives, transform communities, and renew the church. Every member is expected to return an annual commitment card and give on a regular basis. They can do so through the offering, the website, the convenience of electronic funds transfer, or the mail.

Because Resurrection has the purpose of building a church of deeply committed Christians, we have these new member expectations that include giving:

1. To worship regularly
2. To continue to grow in faith by participating in a small group study
3. To serve God with your hands, by volunteering to serve the congregation, community, and world
4. To give in proportion to your income. (Tithing is the basic goal and for some who can, we encourage giving beyond the tithe.) Every member is expected to return an annual commitment card.
5. To bear witness to faith in Jesus Christ, through word and deed

Bishop Robert Schnase, of the Missouri area of the United Methodist Church, invites congregations to practice fruitful ministry in his book *Five Practices of Fruitful Congregations.*[9] He offers a new theology of stewardship and generosity when he invites us to practice good stewardship so that extravagant generosity results. He defines this practice as a vital sign of Christians who witness an unselfish willingness to give in order to make a positive difference for the purpose of Christ. This type of generosity exceeds all expectations and extends to unexpected results.

For Bishop Schnase, it is not about what you have, how you manage what you have, budgets, or even money; it is ultimately about who you are and who you are to become. It is about faithfulness, discipleship, stewardship, and extravagant generosity. Good stewardship and great generosity demonstrate God's grace that becomes evident in personal and spiritual authenticity.

Stewardship and Generosity Goals

Each year your church can establish special tactical goals. Set new goals every year. These annual goals will support your vision and purpose. A more complete list can be found in the Online Resources.

Here are some examples:

- To teach and interpret the biblical stewardship principles that enable every member to become a disciple of Jesus Christ who is theologically informed, spiritually transformed, and daily living his or her faith

- To articulate the challenge facing the mainline church today in the areas of financial stewardship due to the changing state of our economy in our community, state, and nation, and to call upon our church leaders to respond faithfully

- To increase the number of pledging households each year with a goal of at least 70 percent of our active membership households participating

- To offer a continuum of educational programs that support individuals and families as they grow in their understanding and implementation of biblical financial principles

- To create a culture of stewardship that celebrates joyful giving, demonstrates faithful giving, offers strategic giving, and moves toward missional and sacrificial giving

How to Grow Generosity

Joseph Grenny, in his book *Influencer*,[10] teaches that leadership is all about intentionally influencing people to grow and change. Grenny would argue that positive influence happens when you develop a strategy for growing a culture of generosity in your local church. Growth that is gradual is sustaining.

The reality is that sometimes good behavior may feel bad and bad behavior may feel good without influencing leadership. In other words, acting selfishly may feel good by those motivated by greed, and acting selflessly may feel bad by those motivated by generosity. What makes the difference? Our feelings may work for or against us. Social behavioral studies indicate that people will not change unless they are influenced.

Strategy creates leadership for the future. It must be innovative. The innovative strategy is not managing the present; it is selectively abandoning the past. Strategy responds to changing needs of people and creating the future. Vijay Govindarajan offers an excellent strategic leadership model in his book *The Other Side of Innovation*.[11]

Growing generosity requires a dynamic strategic planning process that happens every year. Year by year growth will result.

It Takes a Team

How can you organize your stewardship team to be more innovative? What new ways can you create that will result in increased giving? This is the challenge every year as we begin planning for the annual stewardship team. For innovative change to result in increased giving, there must be a dedicated leader and a creative campaign team.

Who you select to serve on the leadership team makes all the difference. The project team will be focused on creating a better future, not managing the present. The statement, "We have always done it this way," will not work. The team will need to make room for change by selectively eliminating past practices that did not bring good results.

Govindarajan would also say that there should be two teams. One team should create the new and innovative practices. Another team needs to execute the project. Most churches can take the time to dream, innovate, and create a stewardship campaign to meet the needs of their particular congregation. These churches recruit a team approach. The next chapter will go into much greater detail about the stewardship and generosity team.

Every stewardship campaign can be like a spiritual revival to help people with teaching that informs, inspires, and leads to action and change. Vision becomes reality!

It Takes Time

At Resurrection our discipleship journey is to know, love, and serve God. Our vision for stewardship is also an expression of knowing with our minds, loving with our hearts, and serving with our hands. We teach that giving grows as we know, love, and serve God. Generosity becomes an essential part of the discipleship journey. Generosity really is a result of our commitment to being disciples of Christ for the transformation of the world.

To be candid, few successfully complete this journey. We estimate that in most churches only about 10 percent do so. We also admit that roughly 10–15 percent of the membership never even get started on this journey. The vast majority of members begin the journey but stop short of experiencing the joy of generosity because of other priorities that come before giving to God.

Dr. Walter Russell says, "Generosity is the natural outcome of God working in individuals so that they are conformed to the image of Christ and become generous, as Christ is generous. As a result of this journey, they grow in the grace of giving and will take hold of that which is life indeed (I Timothy 6:19)."[12]

Karl Barth makes this wonderful theological observation: "Grace and gratitude belong together like heaven and earth, grace evokes gratitude like the voice of an echo. Gratitude follows grace as thunder following lightning."[13]

Professor Russell describes the different stages of maturity that we experience on the road to generosity. As children toddling on the road, we give because we see others give (imitation). As we mature, our motivation for giving deepens with our awareness of the needs of others (compassion). There are also those times when we learn to give because others will notice (recognition). Many times in life people sense their absolute dependence upon God. Their motivation for giving becomes more internal (matter of the heart). There is an observation by some that generosity has a strong connection to one's soul. People may ultimately realize that life and faith become more important than selfishness or possessions.

Romans 6:22 puts it this way: "But now that you have been set free from sin and become slaves to God, you have the consequence of a holy life, and the outcome is eternal life."

Henri Nouwen puts it this way: "Gratitude flows from the recognition that who we are and what we have are gifts to be received and shared."

Nouwen goes on to remind us of our vision: "Fund-raising is a form of ministry. It is a way of announcing your vision, and inviting other people into your vision with the resources that are available to them. It is saying, we have a vision that is so exciting that we give you the opportunity to participate in that vision with the resources God has given you and be pleased for that occasion."[14]

Summary

What is your vision for stewardship and generosity? Do you have the courage to cast this vision and teach its values? Casting a vision for such in your church can be the fuel and motivation others need to respond to God's call on their lives to benefit the common good of Christ and the church. It is a long and beautiful journey to creating a culture of generosity in your local church. Be patient. Take your time. Sow seeds of expectation for generosity along the way. Make sure that every year you move forward with greater faith and fruitfulness propelled by your vision. The task of creating a generous community of faith happens as we "creep, crawl, run" toward the fulfillment of our vision and purpose.

Online Resources

Strategic Goals for Stewardship and Generosity

Chapter 3

Creating a Committed Church Community

Herb Mather says, "Stewardship is hard to define. Many church stewardship committees struggle to figure out what in the world they are to do. They hear a mixed message: Stewardship is more than money. But shouldn't the committee do something about financial stewardship?"[1] For too long stewardship focus in the local church has been fuzzy. We need clarity of purpose for our stewardship ministry if the church's financial stewardship ministry is to thrive. This chapter will discuss the essential tasks, attributes, and clear expectations of the stewardship and generosity team. The need for dynamic leadership is also addressed.

While it is helpful to have a broad and holistic understanding of stewardship, it is most important today for the stewardship and generosity team to focus on financial stewardship. The finance committee can appoint this team to make financial stewardship the financial focus. Financial stewardship has never been more essential to fulfilling the mission and vision of the church. Our prayers, presence, and service are vital to our church community. But these are discipleship priorities.

The United Methodist Church 2012 *Book of Discipline* (¶ 258.4) describes the task of the committee on finance to manage all the church's financial needs. They may establish a sub-group or task force that would plan, strategize, and implement ways to generate financial resources for mission and ministries of local churches and beyond. It goes on to call for creative ways to turn congregations into tithing congregations with an attitude of generosity. The chairperson of the ministry group on stewardship is now to become a member of the committee on finance. Adding the stewardship chairperson gives stewardship greater visibility and priority. This enhanced leadership role can bring vitality to giving.

I believe the stewardship and generosity team should be of greater priority than a sub-group or a task force. Other denominations design and organize their stewardship teams as an essential partner in the total ministry of the local church. In some churches the chair of the stewardship and generosity team has a voice and vote on the finance committee and the church council. Stewardship then has an impact on every aspect of ministry. Stewardship needs the support of the congregation's leadership in all areas. When this happens financial giving is a strong vital sign of your church's future health that produces greater results.

A Compelling Need

I would encourage pastors and church leaders to consider organizational ways to improve stewardship and generosity in order to improve the overall health of your church's ministry and mission. This begins by recruiting key leaders. Many churches today that recognize this growing need hire staff to manage this ministry of stewardship and generosity. The results in most cases are amazing. I have consulted with many local churches that are seeing measurable benefits by making stewardship and generosity a greater leadership priority! For example, during the last ten years the role of executive pastor of generosity at the United Methodist Church of the Resurrection has been proven necessary and most beneficial. Our community values the vital role of stewardship and generosity.

In the church we may not want to talk about competition from other nonprofit organizations or ministries, but the reality is that we must. We need to think seriously about what the church offers that brings a positive competitive advantage in every community that we serve. What is it that the church alone can provide? What impact and competitive difference can the church make in your community?

What is it that can propel the church into vital church with impactful ministries and mission? There is a competitive advantage for the church, but we often fail to recognize it. When we do not recognize that there are many nonprofit organizations competing for the charitable dollar, we miss our potential.

I recently reviewed the new book from *New York Times* best-selling author Patrick Lencioni, *The Advantage*.[2] He argues that the seminal difference between successful companies and mediocre ones has little to do with what they know and how smart they are and more to do with how healthy they are. This is also true for nonprofit organizations and local churches.

Your church, too, may fail to ask how it can be healthier. Simply put, Lencioni would say that when a church is healthy, consistent, and complete, its leadership, operations, and culture are unified. The vision, purpose, and mission of the church become dynamic drivers that produce measureable results when the church is healthy.

Lencioni states that healthy organizations outperform their counterparts, are free of politics and confusion, and provide an environment where leaders never want to leave. Why can't the same be true for the church? What prescriptions are necessary for your church to become healthier? How can we best maximize our church's potential?

One area of the local church that most needs to be healthier is the financial stewardship ministry. In most churches the stewardship and generosity ministry is not a leadership priority. This is in need of attention now! The stewardship and generosity ministry is foundational to all the church is called to do. It is no longer possible to neglect the financial stewardship needs and continue to be a healthy church.

This chapter provides a model of a proven stewardship and generosity team that can enhance giving in new ways. Begin to think of ways this model can be adapted for your local church. Making leadership a priority can maximize generosity and bring excitement and support to the total DNA of your church.

Overcome Anxiety about Money

Many pastors and stewardship leaders are caught up in anxiety around money. Fear and other mixed emotions seem to overcome their ability to give financial leadership. I believe we can find encouragement when we face our fears and begin to celebrate generosity and expand the role and impact of the stewardship ministry. Begin by praying about your thoughts and feelings about asking others to give money for ministry needs.

" 'Don't let anyone lose courage because of this Philistine!' David told Saul. 'I, your servant, will go out and fight him!' " (1 Sam 17:32). We all have giants to face and defeat. He knew that before we can defeat those giant challenges we have to face them directly. I like what Max Lucado says: "Let God thought outnumber your giant thoughts. Focus on the giant and you will stumble. Focus on God and the giant will tumble."[3] Leadership with courage and conviction will develop a strong stewardship program.

Simple but Essential Tasks

The first task of today's stewardship and generosity team is to teach ways that our members can practice better financial stewardship of their own resources. People want to know the answers to the following questions:

- How can we learn how to better manage our money?
- How can we save more?
- How can we eliminate personal debt?
- Why is it important to know and practice budgeting?
- What is tithing and proportional giving to God?
- How can I be more generous?
- What are some of the key biblical teachings about giving?

The second task of today's stewardship and generosity team is to develop strategic ways to encourage giving. The team can begin by asking strategic questions. For example:

- Do we offer financial management classes that are biblically based?
- Do we celebrate the generosity of our people on a regular basis in worship?
- Do we ask our people to pray for discernment before they give?
- Do we give thanks to donors in a timely and personal way?

The third task of today's stewardship and generosity team is to teach the spiritual and biblical ministry values that help members grow in their giving as an act of worship and a joyful witness. Both those who ask and those who give grow in God's grace.

Henri Nouwen reminds us in his book *A Spirituality of Fundraising* that fundraising ministry is to be grounded in prayer and undertaken in gratitude. First Peter 4:10 puts it this way: "And serve each other according to the gift each person has received, as good managers of God's diverse gifts." Nouwen adds, "Fundraising is also a call to conversion. And this call comes to both those who seek funds and those who have funds. Whether we are asking for money or giving money we are drawn together by God, who is about to do a new thing through our collaboration."[4]

At Church of the Resurrection our stewardship team sponsors classes and workshops. Graduates of financial classes like Good Sense, Crown Financial, or Financial Peace University give an average of 7 percent to their church and charity as compared to the 2 percent national average. People who understand the connection between faith and money are more generous.

We have now had well over twenty-five hundred attend one of our financial stewardship classes in the last ten years. We also know that those who volunteered in the last twelve months donate ten times more than non-volunteers. Involvement is a vital indicator of generosity. We have discovered that those who are active members of small groups, classes, and leadership groups donate eight to ten times more to our church than those who do not get involved. Involvement of members and visitors is the key to creating a community of generosity.

Key Attributes of the Stewardship and Generosity Team

When organizing your stewardship team be sure to recruit team leaders who demonstrate the following five attributes:

1. Equips Others

How can we best equip non- and nominal Christians to respond to God's call of discipleship, stewardship, and generosity? In Romans 12, Paul talks about being members of the body of Christ and how our spiritual gifts can equip members to build up the church. The gifts of prophecy, ministry, teaching, exhortation, generosity, leadership, and compassion are all needed. The stewardship team can focus on teaching others in the gift and practice of generosity.

Again, the first task of the stewardship and generosity team is to teach and equip all members to be good money managers. Wesley's teaching on the matters of money included helping people earn, save, and give! Before people can give, they must be able to earn, eliminate debt, waste less, and save more.

2. Builds Trust

"Trust in the Lord with all your heart; don't rely on your own intelligence. Know him in all your paths, and he will keep your ways straight" (Prov 3:5-6).

The financial committee and stewardship and generosity team members must be trustworthy. Members of the congregation see this attribute as essential. People put their trust in the integrity of those responsible for the financial stewardship of the church.

Financial leaders, including the pastors and staff, can build trust when systems of accountability, support, and encouragement are in place. Confidentiality is absolutely needed by all who handle finances.

3. Champions Generosity

Members of the stewardship and generosity team lead by example in their giving. They practice tithing or are willing to work toward the tithe as their giving goal. They will demonstrate the joy of generosity in their tithes and offerings.

Paul writes about the wonderful example of the Macedonians' generosity in 2 Corinthians 8:1-2: "Brothers and sisters, we want to let you know about the grace of God that was given to the churches of Macedonia. While they were being tested by many problems, their extra amount of happiness and their extreme poverty resulted in a surplus of rich generosity."

4. Offers Faithful Examples

Team members demonstrate their personal commitment to Christ and the church. They are committed to our church's purpose and practice regular attendance in worship. They are able to work with others and are open for God's direction on their lives.

Colossians 3:23-24 says, "Whatever you do, do it from the heart for the Lord and not for people. You know that you will receive an inheritance as a reward. You serve the Lord Christ."

5. Creates a Focus on Spiritual Transformation

Team members are committed to the growth and spiritual transformation of all the members and visitors of the church. They are eager and open to sharing and promoting testimonies on the joy of generosity in a way that also demonstrates humility so that lives are changed. It is a matter of the heart!

We know that all too often Christians may report that God has given them a changed heart and mind, but their response has not demonstrated a changed life. We ask ourselves how we can help Christians with the transformative power of the gospel so that they can know the joy of a changed life of discipleship and stewardship.

"Don't be conformed to the patterns of this world, but be transformed by the renewing of your minds so that you can figure out what God's will is—what is good and pleasing and mature" (Rom 12:2).

Leadership Staffing Is Essential

Throughout my forty years of ministry, I have had the privilege of working with four outstanding local church stewardship teams. I can tell you that these key leaders have made all the difference. In small, medium, large, and very large churches, the lay leaders and stewardship team chairpersons have given outstanding leadership that resulted in spiritual and financial growth at the four churches I have served. Recruit the best team leader you can find. Pastors who work directly with the team chairperson will bring great results.

When searching for outstanding team leaders, it is helpful to have a prepared ministry description. A job description for the chair of the stewardship team can be found in the Online Resources.

Team Member Roles and Responsibilities

Team members also need to know what is expected. Ask yourself what your expectations are for each year. Here are the twenty most important team tasks:

1. To work in a collaborative way to support the efforts of the finance committee, senior pastor, and staff in developing, managing, and evaluating the annual operating campaign
2. To assist in communicating, teaching, and witnessing financial stewardship and provide opportunities for people to participate in their understanding and practice of financial stewardship

3. To support, oversee, and evaluate Financial Peace University, the Legacy Journey, and other year-round stewardship education classes
4. To work in a supportive role with your endowment committee to promote legacy giving. Estate planning is designed to help members better prepare for the second half of their lives through financial planning
5. To study and grow in the biblical understanding of financial stewardship and generosity
6. To help members recognize the joy of generosity that results in fulfilling your church's purpose, vision, and journey
7. To offer ways to celebrate the results of generosity through stories, testimony, interviews, or video and other social media
8. To analyze and present trends in giving so that financial church leaders can be advised
9. To encourage new ways to reach different generations for greater generosity
10. To create a culture of generosity so that every area of ministry and mission will teach and encourage good stewardship that propels great generosity
11. To educate every member to practice good personal stewardship as part of his or her spiritual life. Help people experience the joy of giving!
12. To encourage new members to be joyful, grateful givers and to return a new member commitment card
13. To continue to grow the number of members who return an annual commitment card and grow in their giving, as able
14. To teach biblical truths about giving to God
15. To follow John Wesley's admonition: "Gain all you can, save all you can, and give all you can."[5] In Wesley's sermon 50, "The Use of Money," he taught the timeless truth that if we spent less, saved more, and managed our money well, there would be more to give and use for God's purposes
16. To study the latest US trends in religious giving and make recommendations to our church leaders. Understand how different generations need unique communication appeals for generous giving. The annual USA Giving Report offers great insight
17. To analyze the annual operating campaign and share observations and recommendations to the senior pastor, the financial committee, and church leaders

18. To assist the stewardship pastor in the preparation of an annual report for the finance committee and church council. This report could include the following:

    - Review of the previous year's operating campaign
    - Proposals for the upcoming sermon series to support the stewardship campaign
    - A report on Financial Peace University and all other financial classes
    - An update on new member commitment card response levels
    - Recommendations based on the annual stewardship segmented survey

19. To review and evaluate the key objectives each year
20. To establish key objectives for each year and monitor such at each meeting

Setting Long-Range Strategic Stewardship Goals

Setting annual goals for your stewardship and generosity ministry is very important to help create focus and energy. Strategic planning can best be developed with three years in mind; but whether it is a one-year plan or a three-year plan, goals need to be specific, measurable, assignable, realistic, and time-related. These goals will need the annual support of the finance team and church council.

These goals will be a result of a brainstorming session but will need to be refined with those who are going to be executing these goals before final decisions and approvals are made. For best results, ownership of goals is important. Every year it is helpful to evaluate the previous year and then modify your strategic goals for the new year, if necessary.

It is recommended that you limit your strategic goals to three to four per year. Too few goals will not generate the leadership dynamic you need, and too many will be frustrating to all involved. These goals can also become part of the pastor's or staff's professional annual goal-setting process.

Specific goals can identify those areas of your ministry that need improvement. Measurable ways of quantifying the progress or results are essential for evaluation. Always ask, "Who will be responsible for the project?" Realistic expectations are important, and yet the expectations should encourage risk. Failure should not be punished. Add time-related schedules to keep moving us forward toward completion or at least give us a sense of accomplishment.

Here are some sample goals from Resurrection's stewardship and generosity ministry:

To teach and interpret the biblical stewardship principles that enable every member to become a disciple of Jesus Christ who is theologically informed, spiritually transformed, and daily living their faith.

To celebrate that God "gives life, breath, and everything else," so that "in God we live, move, and exist." God is the giver of all good gifts (Acts 17:25, 28)!

To teach Christian stewardship as the faithful practice of systematic giving of our tithes and offerings. Every member is invited to give a percentage of their income with the tithe (10 percent) as a goal. We seek to find creative ways to become a tithing congregation.

Generosity and Stewardship Team—Annual Objectives

The purpose of the generosity and stewardship team is to build a Christian community where non-religious and nominally religious people are becoming deeply committed Christians.

The team's stewardship mission is to encourage and celebrate God's many blessings of time, talent, financial gifts, and service, which we manage wisely and give gratefully with the joy of generosity.

It is critically important that the stewardship and generosity mission support the church's purpose to create a culture of generosity.

At each stewardship meeting we review our progress on these objectives:

1. Teaching our members the biblical principles of stewardship and generosity:
    - Financial Peace University—two classes each semester
    - Financial Peace University for Single Women—one class each semester
    - Budget Planning Workshops—one class each semester
    - Legacy Journey Study—two classes each year
2. Inviting our members to become deeply committed Christians by practicing percentage giving with tithing becoming the goal:
    - Distribute giving guides at the annual campaign
    - Provide stewardship and generosity materials for stewardship campaign
    - Use new member giving guides at new member coffee meetings
    - Keep website information up to date

3. Assisting others for better personal stewardship and financial management by offering seminars, coaching, small group studies, and other events:

- Pre-Retirement Seminars
- Estate Planning Workshops
- Women's Estate Planning Workshops
- Social Security Workshops
- Medicare Workshops
- Pre-retirement Bible study curriculum

4. Giving leadership and support of our annual stewardship education and financial operating and capital campaigns:

- Serve during campaigns
- Offer creative and new ideas to help people in money management
- Evaluate campaigns and follow-up programs

5. Celebrating the generosity of our congregation by sharing stories and testimonies:

- Quarterly financial statement—newsletter (print/digital)
- Daily testimonies are included in our Grow, Pray, and Study Guide

6. Supporting planned giving as members remember the church in their estate and IRA gifting

7. Promoting and support new member giving:

- Provide information at the New Member Coffee with Pastor events—five/six times per year
- Send thank-you letters to those who return a commitment card
- Send follow-up invitation letters to those non-responders

How to Help New Members Give Generously

One of the most important aspects of our stewardship ministry at Resurrection is finding relevant ways to help and encourage new members to become generous givers. Our stewardship team takes an active role at our new member orientation programs that we call "Coffee with the Pastor."

The majority of our new members are non- or nominal Christians who have not been practicing tithing or percentage giving with the tithe as a goal. The money issue may have been a major obstacle to joining. Each new member knows that there are new member expectations and one of them is that every member will return an annual commitment card. We want our members to practice percentage giving with the 10 percent tithe being the annual giving goal. We know that if our new members give they can feel levels of partnership and responsibility. So we encourage new members to start somewhere and strive to increase their giving each year with 10 percent as the goal in giving.

People who get plugged into and involved with the church will financially support your ministries. Send a personal thank-you letter when your records indicate you have received a first-time gift. Saying thank you can really encourage new members and visitors.

A new member giving guide brochure, along with a new member commitment card, is part of the information packet distributed at the Coffee with the Pastor. The senior pastor, Adam Hamilton, shares his tithing testimony and reviews our giving expectations. The executive pastor of generosity is introduced and is available to greet new members. Our stewardship team staff and volunteers have an information table.

New members who are ready to return a commitment card do so at the stewardship information table. Those who are not ready to return a card can mail it in the envelope provided, or place it in the worship offering plate. Nearly 70 percent of our new members return a new member commitment card at the time they join the church.

A catalyst to getting new members to start returning a commitment card is offered when we receive their card. We give or send them a thank-you letter and a coupon to redeem at our church book store. They also receive a new study Bible designed to aid them for years to come.

Promote Financial Stewardship Classes

Our senior pastor, Adam Hamilton, in his book *Enough*,[6] has helped thousands of pastors and churches discover the joy of generosity through simplicity. There is a very helpful *Enough Stewardship Program Guide*[7] that describes every aspect of creating the culture of generosity and joy in your local church.

People today want to talk about money. It is no longer the "elephant in the middle of the room." Since the Great Recession this interest in helping visitors and members with financial planning has been most fruitful. Our preaching and teaching stewardship helps people reset their priorities. People are encouraged to get out of debt, save more, and give more. People at all economic levels have great need and interest in learning to be better money managers.

Many participants have taken Dave Ramsey's Financial Peace University course at Resurrection. Nearly one-third of those are non-members. Everyone wants help regardless of their economic situation. We need financial security in an uncertain financial world. That sense of security can be built upon biblical principles of stewardship. Our Stewardship Ministry is also sponsoring the Dave Ramsey course called Legacy Journey. It is taught by our pastor of generosity and designed for those who want to develop a financial plan for the second half of life. New members can be encouraged to take stewardship classes along with study programs like Alpha, Disciple Bible Study, and Journey courses.

We know we can help new members by helping them discover where they are going with their spiritual and financial lifestyle. The church can help new Christians grow with incremental steps. We can move them forward in living and giving for Christ. The church will grow and thrive as we preach and teach the good news that really helps people.

An Honest Assessment of Your Stewardship Ministry—A Stewardship Audit

Quantifying generosity and stewardship is a challenge in every church. Yet, it is necessary to know where we are so we can determine where we need to go! There are many different methods for setting the benchmarks. We can certainly learn a lot from other churches to benchmark our goals and objectives.

We also know that every church is different. Our history is different. Churches have different leadership styles and are different theologically. This is why each church needs a measure that best fits them and the context of their demographic community.

The stewardship audit process is valuable because it can improve the culture of generosity in your church! Here are some of the benefits:

- It will inform your decisions about what initiatives or programs in your church could be continued, improved, started, or discontinued.
- It is a great way to make a case for increased leadership resources or funding for your stewardship program.
- It can enable you to strategically look for ways you can improve stewardship and generosity programs.

Once you complete your audit, then do an external audit of factors that influence generosity today in your community. (An in-house audit is available; see Online Resources: "Assessment and Audit of Your Stewardship and Generosity Ministry.")

Conclusion

Build your church community's level of financial commitment and joy. Get started. Keep it simple. Leadership is the key, so recruit the best. Find training opportunities for your leadership. Make a little progress each year. Plant seeds of generosity and watch God cultivate a culture of generosity in your local church. It may take years of faithful stewardship and generosity to make a lasting difference. Celebrate your progress and growth each year. Sustained giving by faithful donors will create a committed faith community!

Online Resources

Stewardship Team Chairperson Job Description

Section II

Insights for Preaching and Worship

Preaching financial stewardship sermons is a difficult task for most preachers. And yet, financial resources for ministry are urgently needed. The challenge facing the church today is economic uncertainty and that most churches are lacking financial resources. Too many people of faith have a worldview of scarcity rather than abundance. We miss the potential for the joy of generosity unless we can understand and overcome many challenges.

Years ago, I was appointed to a thirty-five-hundred-member congregation church with the bishop's admonition: "Clayton, I am going to appoint you to this church so you can you give leadership and build the larger sanctuary that is needed for this church to grow." I have always tried to say yes to my bishop. But my anxiety caused me some hesitation and much prayer.

After I completed my first year of serving this new church, I enrolled in a doctor of ministry program at McCormick School of Theology. The dean, Don Wardlaw, asked me what my greatest challenge was in ministry. I quickly reported my anxiety around preaching financial stewardship. Without hesitating, he said, "Clayton, I want you to do your research and thesis in the area of preaching financial stewardship sermons." So much of the next three chapters are a result of my research, study, and ongoing experience for the last twenty years of my ministry. To this day, I am grateful for Dr. Wardlaw's challenge, which led to the opportunity to overcome one the greatest challenges of ministry for me.

Preachers and seminary students today report financial conflict within themselves. Others may not want to recognize that a problem truly exists. Many pastors today are in debt and lack financial management skills necessary to model good stewardship and generosity. Many churches and some seminaries are now offering courses on money management with great results.

Denominational leaders have reported to me that over half of our pastors have personal financial issues. During a parish leadership seminary course I taught recently, I learned more about the tremendous debt load of many of our seminary students. In many cases debt may prevent pastors or seminary students from being able to give or tithe. In these cases pastors realize that they cannot lead by example. Many desperately wanted help so they can learn how to eliminate their debt. This section will speak to the "preacher within" to discover the preacher's inner conflict and urgency. It will also offer some practical steps and theoretical insights to empower preaching financial stewardship messages that help people with better money management and debt reduction.

There are several helpful theories that will be identified and then examined for those who want to go deeper into the preaching dynamics necessary to be an effective and faithful preacher of financial stewardship sermons. For example, Craddock's theory of indirect communication is thoroughly examined. The practice of self-disclosure is analyzed. Chapter 4 will describe seven aspects that improve the confidence and impact of the preacher's personality on preaching. The goal is to offer help and hope. The Online Resources will provide suggestions and resources for money management courses.

There are also a number of practical skills that I will also identify in the next three chapters. For twenty-five years I served as a senior pastor and preached annual financial stewardship sermons. For the last ten years I have served as an executive pastor of stewardship and generosity. During this time I have studied the financial teaching and preaching style of our senior pastor, Adam Hamilton. I have learned much from Adam's rhetorical gifts and other great preachers over these years that may be of some help to anyone who wants to improve.

David G. Buttrick says, "Rhetoric is a practical wisdom. Though we still read Aristotle's *On Rhetoric* with appreciation, in every age since Aristotle there have been rhetoricians."[1] Buttrick tells us how to speak and how people listen. You can learn how to speak about money with a clear and compelling evangelical style. I would encourage the reader to study the rhetorical preaching style of Adam Hamilton by reading his book *Unleashing the Word*[2] and listening to his online archived sermons at www.cor.org. Deeper insights for preaching and teaching are offered in the next three chapters. Dr. Don Wardlaw, my professor and dean, encouraged seminary students with this statement: "Each of us already has the effective preacher within us that God wants us to become!" One outcome will be the preacher's own growth through the use of self-disclosure and indirect communication theories in preaching. Another recommendation will be the ongoing use of small group support for planning and improving preaching, congregational contextual knowledge, and biblical teaching applications.

Chapter 4

Moving Forward—Six Transformational Steps

Preachers who seek greater self-understanding will be more effective in preaching stewardship sermons. Pastors who have a deeper knowledge of their personality and its impact on the congregation will be more effective. For years I had based my homiletical preparation process on the biblical text and the congregational context. I am now proposing a third homiletic focus. This homiletic tool is the intentional dynamic of the preacher's personality and leadership style. Pastors who seek better self-understanding will honor their urgent task. With greater self-understanding preachers will be more open and honest about the anxiety when faced with preparing and preaching financial stewardship sermons.

My goal is to help you empower your leadership and vision while nurturing trust with your congregation. Most of us need a corrective to feelings of inadequacy, avoidance, and anxiety. Furthermore, I intend to demonstrate how this threefold homiletic model based on the preacher's personality, the congregational ethos, and the biblical teaching can best instruct and inspire the anxious preacher with new effectiveness.

This chapter is based on my own preaching journey, research, and doctor of ministry study in the area of preaching financial stewardship. In the first two years of my research project I recruited a small focus group of key laypeople to help me design a financial sermon series. In the third year I also utilized this model for weekly worship planning sessions with staff. The goal was to help this pastor analyze the congregation's context and need. I could then discover what preaching style would be most effective according to my personality and interpretation of the text.

Again our task is threefold: to better understand the congregation's needs, to know with confidence the biblical imperatives, and to comprehend more fully the role of your personality and its impact. Our biggest challenge is how we best practice self-disclosure that is authentic and inviting.

I will examine the status of preaching financial stewardship sermons today. I will share helpful observations about the practice of preaching by our senior pastor, Adam Hamilton. Adam does an amazing job of self-disclosure. He paints a candid picture for the listener. He talks about his conflict between the anxiety about money and his inner urgency in the preaching stewardship and generosity. There is much to learn about his transparency that demonstrates authenticity to the hearer. Adam has an amazing way of telling his story that invites the listener into his thoughts, feelings, and spiritual values.

Four Proven Theories

Four theories are introduced in this and the next chapter that can help the preacher/teacher improve his or her own self-understanding:

1. Craddock's indirect communication theory
2. Chelune's self-disclosure theory
3. Van der Geest's personality theory of the preacher's posture for preaching
4. Luft's change theory based on small group dynamic

Understanding and applying these time-tested theories will produce practical results. I believe the reader will identify with the validity of these theories.

Times have changed. Preaching what was once an honored, unquestioned, authoritative Word no longer has the same value. It is still important that the Word be heard and that the financial stewardship sermon be addressed to us by the human voice of the preacher. The ultimate purpose of preaching is to draw us near to God as Calvin identified in Ephesians 4:10-13: "God has chosen the voices of a human mouth because God prefers to address us in human fashion in order to draw us near, rather than thunder at us and drive us away."[1]

Today's preacher often experiences preaching as a death-defying act. Barbara Brown Taylor writes so vividly,

> Watching a preacher climb into a pulpit is a lot like watching a tightrope walker climb into the platform as the drum roll begins. The first clears her throat and spreads out her notes; the second loosens his shoulders and stretches out one rosin-soled foot to test the taut rope. Then both step out into the air, trusting everything they have done to prepare for this moment as they surrender themselves to it, counting now on something beyond themselves to help them do what they love and fear and most want to do. If they reach the other side without falling, it is a skill but it is also grace—a benevolent God's decision to let these daredevils tread the high places where ordinary mortals have the good sense not to go.[2]

So how might the preacher walk the tightrope between one's personality and congregational needs? The task of the preacher is to call people to an authentic relationship with God, enabling people to respond faithfully. The premise is that the better a preacher understands him- or herself and others in the congregational context, the more fearlessly he or she walks that tightrope.

Each preacher can begin by answering these key questions: How does the preacher's self-understanding affect the preaching? How can the preacher best be heard? And, how does the preacher preach the word of God to produce a culture of generosity?

Design a New Preaching Model

The preaching model I propose shapes the sermon in several ways. The financial stewardship sermon will authentically deal with the preacher's personality and pathos, the congregation's ethos, and the biblical logos or mandate. This model for preaching financial stewardship sermons will help correct and enhance our current dilemma. To help you design your new preaching/teaching stewardship model, I will offer six steps preachers and teachers can take.

The challenges facing most preachers deserve additional investigation. Where does your congregation rank in giving among churches in your conference? Does the leadership of your church want the average giving per member to increase to enable further growth of the congregation's ministry? Is there general concern that the giving, membership, and attendance have leveled off in recent years? Do you believe that a strong financial stewardship sermon series each year can help move your congregation toward growth?

Most church leaders believe that financial commitment is a valid indicator of spiritual health and prognosis. Every pastor will want to preach the best stewardship sermons possible to bring change, growth, and vision to a congregation that fears decline. The approach to preaching financial stewardship sermons can move from anxiety to urgency, from feelings of inadequacy to hopefulness. Healthy pastors create healthy congregations.

Preaching financial stewardship sermons often suffers from the methodology of direct communication. Craddock's alternative is to use indirect communication that is somewhat open-ended and suggestive. This is especially important when teaching about financial stewardship. Sometimes this indirect approach frees up what the preacher or hearers already know about themselves. It is a dynamic process based on understanding one's faith and personality. Craddock asks a key question: "How can one person communicate the gospel to another?"[3]

Ask yourself: "How can one best preach on my understanding of money to others?"

Our Difficult Dilemma

Preachers report that they want to preach about spiritual needs, not financial needs. Many may falsely conclude that financial stewardship has little to do with our faith and spirituality. Yet every year as we prepare the church budget our reluctance reappears. Our task is to preach biblical stewardship and encourage people to pledge their anticipated giving as a witness of their spiritual commitment.

The world of the preacher testifies to the polarity of urgency and ambiguity in preaching about giving. Many factors create this tension within the preacher and the church. The Apostle Paul understood its tension when he talked about how grace is not the law and yet it fulfills the promise of the law. In preaching stewardship messages, we must encounter both the law and the gospel. We ask, "Should we give out of joy, duty, or both?"

A Madison Avenue advertising agency surveyed unchurched people's impressions of the church. "The problem with the church," respondents said, "is that people are always sad, or they talk about death, or they ask for money."[4] Most preachers do not want to contribute to the stereotype that has lowered public opinion of the church in recent decades. The questionnaire identified many other reasons for reluctance about preaching financial stewardship sermons. Preachers attributed their reluctance to preach about money to people's negative stereotype of the church.

The scandals surrounding the electronic church of the 1980s continue to take a great toll on society's trust of the church's use of finances. Many television evangelists demonstrated a lack of accountability, if not outright greed. They grossly manipulated their listeners and misappropriated funds. Many preachers today fear that they may be identified with the stereotypical electronic evangelist. People heard highly perverted or twisted prosperity theology about money from too many charlatans desiring to manipulate their listeners to give.

The decline of the mainline church also adds to the preacher's paralysis in preaching financial stewardship sermons. Steven Hart and David Krueger report this dilemma of many mainline Protestants: 30 percent of those interviewed viewed their life and work as being separate from their faith; 39 percent see issues as somewhat integrated; and only 25 percent acknowledge that faith and works are essentially integral.[5]

I believe that the preacher's inability to preach an effective stewardship message from the pulpit has created havoc in the church. Signs point in this direction. Many local churches are struggling to survive, and these churches feel little inclination to give money to denominational programs and missions. Furthermore, denominations that formerly had no difficulty funding ministries now face shrinking budgets, staff, and influence. In most churches the preacher and lay leaders may feel intimidated to produce. Preachers motivated by subtle fear, guilt, or even anger, grow empty and frustrated. Fewer people respond and give.[6] A corrective model is needed!

There is hope. The challenge of this chapter also offers opportunities by which preachers can gain greater self-understanding and confidence as they preach sermons about financial stewardship. Where there is hope there is the possibility of new understanding and insight.

I want to offer six steps that can support this threefold thesis: Preachers who seek greater self-understanding will become more effective in preaching stewardship sermons. Preachers can gain a deeper knowledge of their personality and then discover how they can impact the congregational ethos and fulfill the biblical truth. These six steps will empower your preaching. I see evidence of each of these steps in the preaching of Adam Hamilton and many other excellent preachers.

While it has always been imperative to exegete both the scripture and the world of the congregation, I believe it is also vitally important to exegete the internal world of the preacher. We all know that preaching is difficult, yet it can become a joyful and creative task. People today have a greater interest to understand money. Let's take a few steps into the internal world of the preacher as he or she prepares and delivers the sermon.

Step One: Improve Your Self-Understanding

Many preachers responded to my questionnaire that they felt overwhelmed by the task of preaching financial stewardship sermons. Willard Francis Jabusch describes the fear one experiences when preaching: "Sometimes we preachers get discouraged, not so much because of worries concerning content or technique—as important as these are—and not so much because of a congregation that seems unreceptive, but rather because of who we are... preaching has a way of revealing our personal weakness."[7]

In the preaching process, one can become the agent by which God can communicate. At times, our inner struggle about the problem of preaching a financial stewardship message is the very place where the dilemma gives birth to a greater awareness of "the preacher within."

How the preacher forms ideas merits much study in the history of homiletics. How do we understand our experience of inspiration? Why are there different schools of hermeneutics? Different schools of thought have emphasized different aspects of the idea formation because of different personality types. This past century has produced three major schools of thought: Barth and his followers focus on the biblical text for their source. Fosdick and followers focus on the "life situation" of the hearers. Edgar Jackson and his followers focus on the psychological needs of the hearers, based on a scheme of development like that of Maslow or Erickson. I am suggesting that a focus on the personality of the preacher is also essential.

The model that I propose incorporates the theories of Barth, Fosdick, and Jackson and adds my emphasis and corrective based on the self-understanding of the preacher. Ideas are the forms that communicate all that we are and have experienced as we interpret the biblical text. I have come to believe that God can inspire the "preacher within" to give birth to the most loving and creative possibilities of truth. Better self-understanding helps open the door for us to more fully encounter and understand God. Our preaching and teaching then offers an honest and courageous reflection of who we are and whose we are.

Step Two: Use Indirect Communication

I would argue that the preacher gains greater urgency as he or she translates God's Word into a message appropriate for delivery in the sermon. Chartier says this involves a conscious transformation of formed ideas into symbols appropriate for delivery.[8] This process has been a focal point in many homiletical works. The preacher represents and embodies God's message.

H. Grady Davis would argue that an idea has an inherent shape or natural structure that is as unique and individual as each idea.[9] Craddock suggests that the form of the sermon shapes an idea to the way the person thinks.[10] All this points to the dramatic impact that personality can have on preaching.

For example, in the history of my own homiletical development I have grown to appreciate both the art and science of preaching. I seek ways to enhance both the mystery and the mechanics of the preaching task. Due to the anxiety often caused by the need to preach a financial stewardship sermon, I find it easy to default and limit the internal and artistic process needed. It is much easier to turn to a mechanical and deductive approach. Our defenses seem to go up and our creativity seems to go down. This new model for preaching a financial stewardship sermon calls for the preacher to focus closely on the inner thoughts and feelings of the preacher to prevent such a dilemma.

The basic rhetorical problem in preaching financial stewardship is the lack of awareness that a problem exists. In the past, the method or style was considered less important than content and truth. Methodology was reduced to a matter of "how" and thus was less significant than the "what" of proclamation. Often matters of method fall under suspicion.

Too often the only task of a preacher was to discover the truth in scripture and preach that truth to the congregation. This homiletical framework defines the inhibited or limited role of the preacher as one who presents the discoveries of scripture to the congregation. A personality was not even needed! I was told, "Just tell them to tithe!"

When the preacher is pictured in such a limited way, the preacher also assumed a narrow method. Since matters of method and style may come to be seen as unimportant, this method may not be fully examined for its limitations. This method is called direct communication. Direct communication is the language of presenting information, but it does not consider the relational dynamics of the preacher or the congregation.

When this method is used in preaching it creates an illusion that the task of preaching is to pass on information to others. Craddock asks the reader to answer this question: Does this type of preaching change lives? Craddock believes not. He goes on to argue that more than information is needed to enable people to live their Christian lives. "The hardest distance to traverse is from the head to the heart."[11]

I found that this direct communication style can be fatal to the very task of preaching if the teller tries to keep him- or herself out of the sermon. This stems from the assumption that it was the preacher's task to discover the meaning of the scripture and present the truth, and not disclose self to the congregation. After all, one is called to preach the gospel, not oneself. This rhetorical style of preaching may require the preacher to remain distanced from the congregation. If the preacher comes too close, his or her frailties will show through and the message can be tarnished by the messenger. To avoid this, the preacher remains apart from God's people for the sake of the message.

Craddock sees this rhetorical dilemma as fatal to preaching: The Christian faith is communicated from faith to faith: it is a product of intensity, discipline, passion, and pathos.[12] It is necessary for the preacher to move closer to the scripture and to the congregation. The first task of the preacher is not to find something to say to someone but to hear the gospel for him- or herself. The preacher needs to first overhear and appropriate the message for him- or herself. It is in one's self-understanding that the preacher discovers passion!

Step Three: Build Trust

Having moved closer to the pathos of the preacher, let us move even closer to the congregation. The congregation has developed its own ethos of the preacher. The preacher needs to stand close enough that the congregation understands that the preacher will overhear their strengths, struggles, concerns, and joys as well. Indeed the preacher needs to stand with the congregation so the congregation overhears and understands that both are addressing God and being addressed by God. Pastors and stewardship leaders are more effective when they understand the congregation and the congregational needs.

Now let us look at the listener's needs according to Craddock's perspective. The listener assumes that one participates in genuinely Christian communication when one hears the sermon. The point of religious discourse is to reconstruct the human behavior.[13] If passing on information is not changing people, then the listener suffers, though he or she may not know why.

When the listener hears the informational sermon, he or she responds, "Here we go again, I agree, I have heard this before, I know that, or that is interesting."[14] The listener believes he or she has heard the gospel, but there is no change. Financial stewardship sermons call for a deeper dynamic of change of the heart that is trustworthy.

Sometimes direct communication creates confrontation. The preacher's idea that the Holy Spirit will convince the congregation of the truth may lead to the understanding that the preacher must confront people with the gospel. Convincing and confronting may sound noble and prophetic, but they may block listening. They are words of attack. When a listener is attacked a defense is erected. This may take the form of disagreement or disengagement, but in either case he or she no longer hears. This may happen too often in financial stewardship preaching that is confrontational. And we wonder why attendance declines during the financial stewardship season!

For me, direct discourse creates pastoral distance. Distances may result in attack, but also form the illusion of participation that occurs when information is presented and facts are stated. The listener believes he or she has participated in Christian discourse but he or she is really still distanced from the message. The message has not embodied the listener's personhood because it is not embodied within the preacher. Trust does not result.

Step Four: Preach with Biblical Impact

I would argue that method and message must be a good fit. If they are not, scriptural teaching will lose its authority and power. People believe they are hearing the gospel when the authority of the scripture rests in its power to change and transform. So a method that thwarts these changes undermines the scripture's authority and keeps people too distant from the scripture.

I found that the method of direct communication or deductive preaching does not bring the best results in preaching financial stewardship messages because of today's diminished authority of scripture. One solution to the problem of distance is to speak with personal authenticity. Some try to overcome this distance by focusing on the immediacy of scripture: What does it mean to me? What does it say now? How has the biblical truth given me financial freedom from debt?

Transformational preaching happens in the preacher who authentically experiences a change of heart and mind. Sermons that are life changing have been embodied by the preacher and inspired by the logos. Davis speaks to the ultimate biblical goal of preaching:

> The verdict and decision we ought to preach for is itself that radical transformation of which we have been speaking: not a change of opinion but a change of a purpose, not a new fashion of life but a new foundation for existence. If we call for nothing better than moral improvement, we shall get nothing better. If we wish for nothing better, if we believe in nothing better, we shall not even get that.[15]

The preaching task can be supported by liturgy that enhances the biblical theme and brings transformation. In the preparation for worship it would be wise to use a more creative, inductive, and indirect process. Carol Doran and Thomas Troeger offer several dynamic maps and images that are helpful in analyzing worship. For example, they suggest that the Myers-Briggs personality types can bring understanding and greater inclusiveness of personality preference to worship design.[16]

Obviously, people have different ways of interpreting the scriptures. If the preacher's role is to provide a worship experience that is meaningful to a variety of personality types, he or she must first understand the impact of his or her personality upon biblical interpretation. To do that well, the preacher can also be able to understand who it is that is listening. At Resurrection we design our financial stewardship sermon series with the non- and nominal Christian in mind.

The preacher who becomes aware of the impact of his or her personality will also be sensitive to the personality impact and differences of others in worship design.

Preachers addressing more controversial issues like money and materialism must try to understand their personality characteristics to broaden and balance the impact. We began to see our need to demonstrate a more balanced perspective in the preaching task: "We need to develop some of our less favored characteristics if we want to grow more aware and appreciate the value of others whose personality types are different from our own. Such development may even facilitate spiritual growth, encouraging us to pursue some spiritual approaches that we would normally find ineffective."[17]

The biblical interpretation and homiletic process I suggest is motivated by a threefold goal: to understand the text, to understand the listener's context, and to seek a greater self-understanding in the preacher. In this way the preaching can speak with greater impact.

The preacher's task is to model a theological process of biblical faith seeking understanding. The congregation's identity and vision will then grow to greater commitment of the church's vision. This vision process opens a new horizon of excitement and hope. The biblical focus can then be proclaimed and modeled by the preacher and other worship leaders. For example, when the preacher's self-understanding of the church's vision and the biblical text is evident by the congregation there is an authentic and personal connection.

Dr. Craddock is calling for preaching the biblical story that brings change and transformation. This kind of preaching can begin within the personality of the preacher. The preacher must first know his or her story and then be able to witness to that in relation to the biblical story. It is then and only then that the listener may be fully open to the power of the Holy Spirit to bring about an authentic encounter with God. When the Word speaks to you, you can speak to others.

This dimension of the biblical teaching can point to the incarnation of Jesus Christ as the basis for an appropriate form. Jesus Christ is God's revelation incognito. God is present but not self-evident. Seeing and hearing Jesus does not ensure that one confesses faith in him as God's revelation. Jesus is the example of indirect communication from God. Craddock acknowledges that Jesus often speaks clearly and directly.[18] Even in these cases the hearer's personal investment will bring greater impact and change.

Step Five: Preach with Your Ears

When I served as senior pastor of Manchester United Methodist Church, I learned to listen better. I led a three-year project that was enhanced by the small group process. This small group experience did much to aid my self-understanding and my practice of self-disclosure in preaching. The focus of the project helped me better comprehend and integrate the impact of my personality on preaching financial stewardship sermons. I really worked hard to listen.

The genesis of this project was a voice within me crying out for new insights and courage in my preaching life. As I listened I began exploring by asking certain key questions: What can I learn about myself? What posture can help bring me greater confidence and conviction in preaching about money? And how can others help me understand and experience myself and God through the preaching event? How can I really help others?

My project began with support from the parish group process. The small group environment became the testing ground that offered opportunity for the polarities of my anxiety and urgency to be examined. Years later, I continue to meet each week with a small group. I listen, learn, and teach with greater effectiveness. This results in helping me be open and less defensive. Listening provides a corrective point of view.

Using small groups in the preparation of stewardship sermons is most helpful. You can have the benefit of working with a group of six to ten people each week to help you plan and evaluate the sermons. We developed evaluative instruments to distribute to the congregation. The group's task was threefold: to aid in biblical interpretation, to clarify the congregation's needs, and to help the preacher identify personality issues and dynamics. This process helped test my preaching posture and shaped the financial stewardship sermon. The outcome was dramatic. I better understood my strengths and weaknesses.

The benefit of this focus group helped me to develop a climate of openness. Group members encouraged greater use of self-disclosure in preaching. Each group evaluated me in a way that helped me better see myself. Self-disclosure was identified as the dynamic that could best help me experience the impact of my personality on preaching.

The primary focus of the group process was to help the preacher better understand self in relation to the congregation. Each self-disclosure situation includes three basic elements: the disclosing self, the subject matter and purpose of the text, and the intended target of the stewardship sermon series. What are my doubts, wonders, and beliefs?

It is helpful to teach others that preaching is threefold. Preaching can demonstrate your self-understanding, can be God's revelation in Jesus Christ through the biblical logos, and can help the preacher better connect with the congregational ethos. One member of the parish group stated that preaching can be the key to the preacher's and the congregation's self-understanding and God's revelation in Christ. Preaching does offer a way to deepen commitment to stewardship as people learn to manage their money better, save more, reduce debt, and give more. Others in the parish group confirmed this basic assumption. It became evident that the preacher's self-disclosure enhanced this process. The listeners knew the preacher understood their needs with authenticity.

George Chelune's definition and theory of self-disclosure helps: "It is the free and intentional self-manifestation to another so that the other discovers something unknown about the disclosure."[19] This builds connection and identification with the listener!

Using self-disclosure in my preaching was exciting and challenging. I felt as though I was able to develop a deeper relationship or intimacy with the listeners. Preachers need to know and be known, to hear and be heard, to understand and be understood: "This drive toward sharing the self focuses on the human need to care and to be cared for, to be involved and loved, and to cross the normal barriers of defensiveness and to enter the space where we are most truly ourselves."[20]

The opportunity for deeper trust in relationships became an important outcome of the preacher's use of a small group. People disclose in every encounter with another. I find this theory and practice particularly helpful in my experience with worship planning with staff and lay leaders. I have learned to preach with my ears. I take time to really listen.

I expanded this theory of self-understanding to include others when I developed a four-week series of sermons on the stewardship of spiritual gifts and abilities. This sermon series offered a new slant on stewardship. Each was encouraged to discover and then deploy his or her gift. A great deal of interest was generated in the focus group and the congregation, resulting in a greater self-understanding by the preacher and the people. Members of the group were asked, "What impact has this experience had on you?" One of the group reported, "I feel blessed to have had an opportunity to see a glimpse of the real heart of a man who desperately wants to serve his God. It has made me realize that his love for this congregation is a vital part of the ministry of this church—that each member should feel a commitment to the same loving concern and be willing to help."

Another member added, "The whole experience was enlightening and exciting."

A third member said, "I believe the subject of personal spiritual gifts was unique for a sermon series, and quite valuable to our efforts to live closer to the Lord in everyday life."

Step Six: Evaluate Every Stewardship Campaign

Following this stewardship campaign, an opinion survey was mailed to those households that pledged. Of 864 surveys mailed, 209 (24 percent) were returned. One particular question was asked to determine what motivates people in their financial giving: "In your opinion which of the following helped you most to make your decision about your financial gift this year?"

More than half of the people who responded to the survey said they pledged because of their personal relationship with God, not because of any particular component of the campaign. Less than one-fifth of respondents indicated that they gave because of their understanding of the church's need. Less than one-third of the people who responded indicated that their prime consideration was their financial situation.

Understanding of the importance of congregational ethos also grew through small group reflection. Luft notes the primary importance of two key questions: How do I feel about the speaker? How does the speaker feel about me?[21] These relational questions are vital in communication with your congregation to help build more intimacy and trust.

From the biblical perspective this drive toward intimacy reflects our created nature. Intimacy is one of our deeper human needs.[22] The opportunity for trust in relationships is an important outcome that can be evaluated by levels of financial commitment.

The need for effective communication encourages us to understand the dynamics of our personality and spiritual gifts. Self-disclosure effectively created a climate of openness, trust, empathy, and acceptance. In each financial campaign we can evaluate the sermons. Discover the benefits of making self-disclosure a pastoral resource for the preaching task. John R. Claypool states: "The Christian preacher has an awesome task to perform. He or she must attempt to do far more than simply move people around at a level of behavior. Our task is to re-establish trust at the deepest level, to participate in the miracle of primal reconciliation."[23]

Evaluate the threefold task that is foundational to your preaching and teaching leadership. Find clarity of purpose as you better understand yourself, your congregation, and God's Word. Redesign your preparation for worship based upon these six steps. Help your congregation experience greater joy through generosity.

Online Resources

Teaching Key Biblical Principles

Chapter 5

Fast-Forward—Seven Insights That Propel Preaching

A number of years ago I mailed a brief stewardship questionnaire to 125 preachers, of whom 77 responded. The high level of response demonstrated great interest and the results validated my doctor of ministry research. I continue to ask these questions to those who ask my help and consultation on preaching stewardship sermon series.

The questionnaire asked three brief questions:

1. How many sermons do you preach each year that deal with financial stewardship?
2. How do you feel about preaching financial stewardship sermons?
3. Please give me a brief example of an effective financial stewardship sermon you have preached, and the role you feel your personality played on its preparation and delivery.

The results of this survey varied as individual differences were evident. However, there were common observations that demonstrated the obvious impact of the preacher's personality. Preachers told of sermons that reflected their personality as well as their theology. Their responses verified the difficult challenge of preaching on stewardship. The questionnaires indicated that preachers struggle with their own passion and fears around the task of preaching financial stewardship sermons. This conflict can find resolution for those who seek honest self-understanding to become more effective in preaching sermons on financial stewardship. I offer a rationale by Hans van der Geest to support my observations.

Richard Lischer states that the best classic study that is rigorously restricted to the effect on the listener of the preacher's personality through the sermon was written by Swiss theologian Hans van der Geest.[1] Therefore, this chapter is designed to fast-forward your understanding of the impact of the preacher's personality on preaching financial stewardship sermons. To develop relevant insights I will adapt and update van der Geest's rationale:[2]

1. The clearer the preacher's sense of call and vision, the greater the preacher's confidence.
2. Preaching financial stewardship sermons calls forth a feeling of responsibility to help people better manage money and experience the joy of generosity.
3. The preacher can benefit from understanding his or her own personality strengths and weaknesses.
4. The preacher can model for others a lifestyle of self-giving and authenticity.
5. The theory and practice of indirect communication help the preacher stand in belief or unbelief.
6. The preacher's task to clarify the sermon's purpose is difficult because one must "walk the tightrope" of knowing when to lead and when to leave alone.
7. Small group process that supports self-disclosure helps the preacher perform the task more decisively and less presumptuously.

Van der Geest isolates an important dimension of effective preaching: the hearer's trust of the preacher. This trust is derived largely from the wholeness and depth of the preacher's personality and leadership style.

Van der Geest analyzes the relationship between the preacher's concrete modes of behavior and his or her personality. He promotes a clinical model for training preachers that takes into account their unique gifts and the impact of each preacher's personality. His study originates from a wealth of theological and practical wisdom that comes from an empirical base of two hundred worship services and interviews with parishioners.

It will be very helpful to take a closer look at each of the seven insights of effective preaching. Yet, Clyde Fant offers a helpful warning in this regard: "Listing character traits needed by the preacher is as exactly as futile as listing the attributes of God, no matter how time honored the practice. God cannot be described by any list of attributes, no matter how exhaustive the list. Neither can the human personality."[3]

Insight One: Sense of Calling

First, van der Geest describes the importance of a sense of calling. He points out that when God wishes the word proclaimed, God does not exclude the possibility that the proclaimer genuinely wants the job. I believe my calling was definitely connected to the task of preaching the financial stewardship message. I had an experience in which I felt personally addressed and engaged by the gospel and was called to proclaim it. Any preacher is crippled without a conscious sense of being called especially when the preaching task is difficult.

The preacher within awakens when touched inwardly by the gospel and then is motivated outwardly to give voice to that inner motivation. When the preacher feels personally moved, he or she will be more able to move the listener. This is indispensable for awakening trust in the listeners. Our calling by God offers challenge and opportunity.

Insight Two: Feeling of Responsibility

Another key to understanding the impact of the preacher's personality has to do with the feeling of responsibility. The study of personality development reveals that people learn to become independent, but they also learn to accept responsibility for others. Obviously, accepting responsibility for others is more difficult than being responsible for yourself.

A responsible preacher tries to discover the intent of the biblical passage and be responsible in the proclamation. The responsible preacher does not strive always to make listeners feel good but rather shows them realistic ways to respond to difficult challenges with the good news. That is, if the preacher's personality is dependable, he or she can awaken feelings of security in the congregation and increase the sense of responsibility among the listeners.

Insight Three: Being in Touch with Self

One of the most important keys to understanding the preacher's personality and its impact on preaching is the extent to which that preacher seeks contact with self. In other words, the better I know myself, the more authentic my preaching can become. Only then can I dare to disclose myself and trust more fully in God and others. This trust is an essential dynamic in preaching financial stewardship sermons. It is true that the preacher can awaken deep experiences in others insofar as he or she is able to reach them in him- or herself. Some of the best sermons preached result from intense prayer and deep reflection. Therefore, being in touch with oneself is decisive in preparing and preaching the financial stewardship sermon.

Insight Four: Giving of Oneself

Another key to understanding the impact of the preacher's personality is in the dynamic of giving one's self. Van der Geest points out that anyone seeking community with others is self-giving toward them. Obviously some people have trouble giving of themselves. The difficulty comes with too much reserve, and this is demonstrated in various ways. Intellectualism is a notorious form of reserve. Here one speaks to others only rationally and risks little vulnerability. The intellectual may also speak in a superior way that can bring closed rather than open response. Preachers who demonstrate the intellectual, superior personality also demonstrate few mistakes. In many ways, this type of preaching may inhibit financial giving because people feel insecure due to their own perceived inadequacy.

An intense awareness of the internal and external worlds of the preacher and the listener is an important dynamic of self-surrender. God's promises require surrender. We can trust in God's capacity to provide for our needs. Van der Geest calls for a balance that can bring trust and psychosomatic unity. In other words, we discover our strengths in our weaknesses.

The preacher can reduce the dread of preaching financial giving and witness joy. Joy is found when people celebrate their responsibility. When the preacher demonstrates through his or her self-surrender the giving of oneself, others follow that example. The joy of giving results within the preacher and then the listener!

Insight Five: Standing in Belief or Unbelief

Another key characteristic is summed up as standing in belief or with unbelief. For some it is hard to decide whether it is more difficult to cope with belief or unbelief. Standing in belief in Christ means surrendering. That surrender comes at great cost. One has to give up many secure habits. When one consciously admits doubt and unbelief, one demonstrates a feeling of security that brings ultimate trust in God.

It is that dynamic tension between belief and unbelief that can empower the proclamation. The preacher who models the questioning listener for the congregation gains credibility with others who struggle with their experience of questioning. Preachers' honest confessions are especially effective as people realize that financial giving is an outward witness of trust resulting from belief or unbelief.

Insight Six: Leading and Leaving Alone

Van der Geest points out that good rapport with one's congregation is essential. It is also decisively important for any preacher to find the proper rhythm between leading the congregation and leaving them alone. The personality who can only lead becomes a despot. Someone who only lets the congregation become uninvolved lacks leadership. One finds the dynamic of leadership in the dynamic relationship between these two contrasting positions as the preacher walks the tightrope.

The task of preaching requires that the preacher present the truth and leave some things open to God's mystery and conjecture. Can a preacher portray accurately enough to be dramatically vivid and yet vaguely enough for the listeners to be challenged inwardly to their own faith journeys? This is possible when the preacher begins with a clear purpose statement for the sermon that is honest about what the sermon can and cannot do.

A preacher who leads too gladly will tend to narrate too thoroughly and become theatrical. The key to preaching involves that vital balance between too much and too little instruction, especially about financial stewardship. For example, people today want and need instruction about the wise use of money more than they want to be compelled to give. Since the 2008 Great Recession some of the most effective preaching has been focused on helping people be honest about themselves. When people are honest, they can reduce debt, save more, and live within their means. They become better stewards of their own resources and learn that good stewardship empowers great generosity.

Insight Seven: Performing the Task Decisively and Without Presumption

The final insight that propels us forward is that we must preach decisively and without presumption. Here we claim our calling and its importance in the personality and the pulpit. In a worship service we attend to existential matters in which there is truly no hierarchy. We all relate to God's calling, but with different psychological temperaments.

Nevertheless, the preacher conducts the service and the listeners respond. This may develop into a conflict between the worshipper and the preacher. It is important that the preacher apprehends this authority from the perspective of an adult ego and not a parent ego. For his or her feeling of identity, the preacher must find a proper balance. Presumptuousness may arise when preachers identify too strongly with the biblical text, as if the gospel is no longer scandalous for them. Preachers who overestimate their function abuse the pulpit. Likewise, preachers cannot underestimate their effect when they are decisive.

We may never fully realize how these dimensions of personality have affected preaching. However, van der Geest does offer valid models. These serve as points of orientation in which the preacher can exercise caution, concern, and confidence. In approaching the difficult task of preaching financial stewardship sermons, the seven insights I have discussed are vitally important to changing the preacher's posture and effect.

Applications of These Insights

1. Begin by Evaluating Your Preaching and Leadership Style

Stewardship sermons can take on a different shape. Is self-disclosure of the preacher evident and intentional in your message? Does the sermon invite the congregation to overhear the text and the preacher? Is there greater intimacy? Is your style less confrontational and direct? Is communication open and indirect? Is the purpose statement of the sermon embodied in the preacher? Does the dynamic of self-disclosure empower the preaching and shape the sermon with authenticity? The listener not only enters into the world of the preacher but also gains greater self-understanding when these questions are answered in the affirmative.

2. Remember Self-Disclosure Can Be Transformational

Leadership calls for change. In the field of self-disclosure, research has grown dramatically. There is greater interest in hearing from the preacher's thoughts and feelings. Today's moral climate in our conflicted culture calls the preacher to be a voice for God by reflecting one's personal values and vision. The church needs our best. Now more than ever before, preaching with authenticity and self-closure matters!

Perhaps the most enduring definition of preaching with the practice of self-disclosure comes from Philip Brooks, who says, "Preaching is the communication of truth through personality."[4] This definition has influenced homiletical theory to this day. Many texts considered his definition a springboard. While Philip Brooks emphasizes the personality, he does not see "I" statements as a positive element in preaching. He sees how they can be offensive. However, Brooks believes heartfelt personal experience is vital to the sermon.

My own practice and theory demands personal material with no apology or shame. The personal stories vary from lighthearted family incidents to experiences in ministry. Indeed, the materials that focus on one's personal experience help the people hear more effectively. They are allowed to overhear instead of being confronted directly.

Is there any compelling reason to avoid using self-disclosure in preaching? Obviously some dangers remain. On the other hand, many newer preaching publications say that self-disclosure and understanding the dynamic of personality have become important for vital preaching. The bias against the use of self-disclosure has been viewed as a bias against the possible misuses. When self-disclosure helps people see and experience God, it is effective for preaching. Every preacher can discover the effective preacher within himself or herself that God intends!

In a powerful way, the idea of Jesus Christ as God's self-disclosure adds strength to the argument for its use as a homiletical tool that is in harmony with the self-revelation of Christ himself. The sense that form and content are related provides the principle for many who use self-disclosure in preaching. The form of proclamation empowers the content. The style of the content reflects the personality of the preacher. The preacher's use of self-disclosure brings harmony and self-understanding for both.

3. Share Your Own Leadership Example

Self-disclosure of the preacher's pathos provides a point of identification for the congregation and identification with the preacher. It is an insight into the feelings and struggles of the preacher or even the way he or she has experienced grace or doubt. Self-disclosure moved me in ways that enhanced my faith with a greater sense of authenticity. My stewardship sermons now demonstrate more authenticity than anxiety! I can lead by example.

Our preaching task is to be always aware of the needs of the congregation. While each preacher should grasp the topic of the sermon, the sermon is not for the preacher. It is especially for the congregation. Self-disclosure of the preacher within adds a dynamic to the sermon process because its use will benefit the hearers. I now question each use of the self-disclosure process by asking, "how does this meet the hearer's need to give financially?"

In preaching a financial stewardship message, trust is important for ongoing relationships. Self-disclosure can function as an essential part of the pastor's entire ministry. It is not a tool or technique just for preaching. Rather, it is most effective when used in every facet of the preacher's relationship with the congregation. This will enable the congregation to trust the pastor to be the same person throughout the ministry. A bonding can occur even in a large church. One of Adam Hamilton's greatest gifts in leading and preaching is his use of authentic self-disclosure. For example, his spirituality is transformed as he communicates his deep relationship with God through his own commitment to giving generously.

The preacher's use of self-example in all aspects of his or her work promotes reciprocity from the congregation. For the sermon, this indicates that the use of self-disclosure requires some system to ensure reciprocity. There are many informal settings in the life of the church that may provide an opportunity for response rather than avoidance.

We all know that no ministry is without problems, conflicts, or crises. When self-disclosure has been part of the ongoing relationship between the preacher and the congregation, the higher level of intimacy and frequency of self-disclosure will assist conflict resolution. The pastor who ignores the crisis or problem seems like a liar or at least insincere. When the emotional climate has heightened, the use of self-disclosure can be an appropriate way to clarify the issues. In preaching financial stewardship sermons, the preacher helps by speaking words of grace, especially in conflicted situations, and staff to study the sermon topic and text. Stewardship sermons can in effect be seen as a joint effort of the preacher, staff, and people. It is the church's need, based upon God's need to be served and worshipped, that brings the people and the preacher together and enhances change. This honors congregational ethos!

The preacher may acknowledge to a small group of laity or peers that he or she is struggling with the demands of the text. With help from a small group the preacher can become a "wounded healer" and proclaim the word of God. The preacher becomes vulnerable to his or her inner conflict. This may also affect the listener. When listeners relate to a common struggle, there is identification, intimacy, and growth. This process empowers the congregation and they in turn empower the preacher. This honors the preacher's pathos and example of leadership.

4. Invite the Listener to Think

Another helpful approach links self-disclosure to the genius of Fred Craddock's inductive preaching or what Don Chatfield calls "left-handed preaching."[5] Craddock shows us how to move from deductively preaching legalistically to helping people also experience inductively the story of the gospel.[6] Identifying the gospel story with their story brings people together. Chatfield also invites the listener to journey with the preacher.[7] He emphasizes the common experience of the preacher and the people rather than the differences.

This approach helps bring confidence to the preacher and honors the biblical logos. Paul Scott Wilson challenges the preacher to look within for imagination and to speak for God.[8] We need active biblical language for God today. Who is God? What does God's word have to do with financial stewardship? What does God have to do with my life to make a difference? These are some of the creative questions that inform a biblical theology of preaching. The preacher becomes an active voice for God.

When my dean said to me, "Each of us has within us already the effective preacher God wants us to become," I associated this hope with my self-understanding and God's great commandment to love God, others, and self. This new wonderment unified and validated my psychological and theological understandings about preaching from my heart, mind, and soul.

As a college student majoring in psychology, I had developed what I called a "Christian self-concept." It was based on how one sees oneself, how one sees others seeing oneself, and how one sees God seeing oneself. This concept can offer a sense of threefold empowerment and confidence when preaching or helping others to better understanding of themselves

5. Nurture Revival in Your Heart

I also recall the day I stood in Wesley's Chapel in London. Still a college student, I read the two beautiful gold plaques centered there on the chancel wall: "You shall love your God with all your heart, mind and soul and you shall love your neighbor as yourself." I now have a greater commitment to seek self-understanding through God's love to maximize the dynamic impact of the preacher's personality. I have made three pilgrimages to Wesley's Chapel that have blessed me with a personal revival. Wesley taught us how God's love compels each of us to be our very best.

Today, there are many new stewardship resources to assist the pastor in preparing the stewardship sermon. At a recent Leadership Institute at the Church of the Resurrection, Scott McKenzie said, "Now is the time to reconsider your stewardship message, moving it from financial to spiritual, from mundane to missional, from painful to inspirational!"[9]

Your greatest resource is within you. Your heart can be strangely warmed!

The first sermon I preached as a seminary graduate included a poem that continues to warm my heart to the joy of giving out of love and faith. I meditate on this poem along with Wesley's Covenant Prayer almost daily. I adapted this poem that was first written by Madeline Bridges as "Life's Mirror" after the close of the American Civil War.

There are loyal hearts and spirits brave,
There are souls that are pure and true;
So give the Lord the best you have,
And the best will come back to you:
Give love and love to your heart will flow,
A strength in your utmost need:
And have faith, and a score of hearts,
Will show their faith in your word and deed.

Because preaching financial stewardship sermons is challenging, it can bless us with special moments of insight and inspiration. The distance between your heart and head can diminish. Gain greater courage to preach in ways that reveal your heart as you give voice and proclamation of the personal and social gospel. Trust the power of your leadership and speak with clarity and conviction to meet the challenge of our world in need. Invite others to know and experience the joy of generosity.

Online Resources

Interpretation for Preaching—One Pastor's Process

Chapter 6

Creative Worship Planning

Before you plan worship to support a sermon series on financial stewardship, it is important to pause and assess the financial climate. Understanding the congregation's financial attitude is an essential first step in worship planning. You can begin this process by asking several key questions:

- What do I think the congregation's greatest financial need is today about their personal and cultural situation?
- How can I best witness the scriptures' teachings with greater clarify?
- Can I offer the best practical tools for our congregation to improve their personal and family stewardship and generosity?
- How can these stewardship- and generosity-focused worship services best support the purpose and vision of the church?
- How can I help the congregation experience the biblically based joy of generosity?

The preacher wants to have clarity about his or her purpose for the stewardship sermon series. Will these sermons comfort the afflicted and afflict the comfortable? The preacher's attitude and approach empower the sermon strategy that can clearly connect with the congregation's real-life situation. (The Online Resources will offer sermon series outlines.)

Planning Strategy

Since most preachers are reluctant to preach on giving money, it is critical to begin the preparation with the end in mind. Remind yourself that good preaching is based not on what the preacher wants from the listeners but on what the preacher wants for the listeners. Simply put, our strategy is to help people learn good stewardship and money management practices that will enable them to waste less, save more, and ultimately experience greater joy of generosity. At the end of life we want people to celebrate their legacy of love and faith as witnessed in their living and giving.

Preaching with this strategy in mind empowers the preacher and the listener. The preacher connects with the needs of the listener. The preacher identifies with the listener in such a way that the gospel brings light and new understanding. The worship service offers creative insights for the worshiper. Help and hope are offered.

Because of the challenge of preaching and teaching on stewardship and generosity, strategic worship planning must involve research, knowing the most recent financial trends and attitudes, creative imagination, prayer, reflection, interviews, and intentional tools and resources to aid the listeners. All this is essential to the worship planning process. We want the worship experience to edify and teach.

Worship planning begins with scheduling. When is the best time of the year for a stewardship sermon series for your congregation? What time of the year do people of your congregation most need help and teaching about money management? We have found that the fall is best because people are beginning to think about the year end. They can also begin to plan their budget for the next year. A good stewardship series will aid the budget planning process of the church and members. Our worship attendance in the stewardship sermons series has increased since we started teaching good stewardship and money management practices. People want to learn how to better manage their money so they can eliminate debt, save, and give more. Our stewardship sermon series purpose is not what the church wants from our members but what we want for our members. We strive to help every member with good stewardship practices so they may better experience the joy of generosity.

Planning Tools

We have offered budget planning tools in the stewardship worship series that have been really helpful to our congregation. These resources help people evaluate their financial situation, make improvements, and better plan their budget for the next year. We encourage our members to know what percentage of their income goes to spending, saving, and giving.

The primary purpose to providing financial planning resources that are biblically based is that good stewardship will also help people get out of debt and make giving to God a priority. Some of these worship resources (hard copies or online) may include:

- A simple budget template
- Printed testimonies of those who became debt free, those who know the importance of budgeting, and those who celebrate the joy of generosity

- Information on financial courses
- Key scriptures on money management
- A CD on money and marriage/family
- Materials to help teach children and youth about money
- Bookmarks with key teaching points
- Links to financial planning resources
- Classes offered on budgeting, financial peace, estate planning

Major Paradigm Shift in Worship Planning

Stewardship campaigns are always a time to remind our congregation of our vision to change lives, transform communities through mission, and bring renewal to other churches. We celebrate what God had done through our church the prior year. A video is prepared that tells this story and has testimonies of changed lives due to our congregation's giving. The campaign also recasts our vision of where God was leading our congregation in the next year. Adam's sermons are also designed to inspire people about the biblical concepts of tithing and stewardship. His sermons offer something for the listener's head (understanding), heart (passion), and hands (action).

It should be said that our worship focus (at Resurrection and other churches that I served) is not about giving to a budget. It is about giving to God. It should also be said that we have always practiced stewardship campaigns that use commitment cards as the method by which the donor can respond. Using annual commitment cards continues to be a best practice for most congregations.[1]

The principle of giving to God and the practice of using an annual stewardship commitment card and offering other giving tools that promote and raise expectations continues to be the key to growth in giving. Since 2005 we have seen giving to our annual and capital giving double, strategic giving to missions increase tenfold, and planned giving increase fifty-fold. Our culture of generosity continues to grow as our worship services celebrate generosity.

I would credit Adam's leadership, vision casting, and excellent preaching and teaching with the amazing growth in giving. However, it is Adam's heart for the needs of our congregation that had the most transformative impact. He writes, "As we were planning the annual 2007 campaign, one thing became painfully obvious. There were many people in our congregation who were struggling financially. They were struggling not because they were not making enough money. They were struggling because they were living beyond their means and were saving nothing."[2]

In other words, we have made a paradigm shift from focusing on what the church wants from the members to what the church wants for the members.

Focus on Your Congregation's Need

What we learned from that campaign has helped thousands of congregations who have used Adam's book *Enough* and the *Enough Stewardship Program Guide*. In recent years hundreds of pastors and congregational leaders have asked for additional sermon and worship planning resources. We continue to have meaningful and successful stewardship campaigns as we apply the following worship and sermon planning practices and principles:

1. Base all that you do not on what you want from your people, but on what you want for them.
2. Begin by defining the problem or the felt needs of the congregation.
3. Build your worship services and sermons on the defined needs.
4. Research community resources to learn more about financial problems people are experiencing. What are their worries and concerns?
5. Invite your congregation to come and learn about better money management (stewardship). Even non- and nominal Christians are interested in money management skills.
6. Keep it simple. Encourage people to take simple steps. Help people find joy in simplicity!
7. Find ways to celebrate stories of those who are debt free.
8. Support each key financial principle with a scripture.
9. Use bulletin inserts that offer basic financial planning tools.
10. Help people think about their lifetime financial goals.
11. Use surveys to measure members' stewardship progress.
12. Offer follow-up workshops after worship for those who want more information.
13. Teach about money management. Even though people may resist being asked for money, they still want to hear how to manage it.
14. Tell stories year round of how people redefined their financial goals and put greater priority on giving to change lives for God's glory.
15. Make the offering in every worship service a reminder of the joy of generosity as we worship God in our giving.
16. Make the Christmas Eve offering 100 percent for mission outreach for children in poverty.

17. Celebrate planned giving one weekend a year and tell the story of your endowment program.
18. Observe Memorial Day Weekend and celebrate all the memorial gifts and those remembered in the last year.
19. Celebrate in worship the generosity of your children, youth, and young adults.
20. Use bulletin announcements to offer many different options for people to give food, clothing, Christmas gifts for the needy, and so on.
21. Find creative ways to say thank you to your generous congregation in worship.
22. Give bookmarks and other simple gifts to express appreciation. Every household that returns a commitment card receives a coffee cup with a thank-you card.

Worship That Captures the Imagination

Worship planning aims at bringing glory to God and at the same time to touch the heart, mind, and soul of the worshipers. The pastor's role in worship design is critical for worship that moves people to greater generosity. In his book *A Primer for Preachers*, Ian Pit-Watson describes how sermon and worship design can develop and grow.[3] He describes how the sermon must first grow within the heart, mind, and soul of the preacher. I find this especially true when the worship experience is calling the congregation to respond with financial commitment. Authentic decisions result when God moves the heart, mind, and soul.

The creative use of imagination is very helpful in designing worship services for the financial stewardship series. It is also essential to develop a stewardship worship theme that captures the heart. Here are the creative stewardship campaign themes that have been excellent communication tools for our congregation:

2014 *"The Power of Gratitude in Loving, Giving, and Serving"*

2013 *"The Power of Generosity"*

2012 *"Joy of Generosity"*

2011 *"More than Enough—Financial Wisdom, Courage, and Peace"*

2010 *"Come Dream with Us"*

2009 *"Growing Forward"*

2008 *"Reset: Biblical Wisdom for Challenging Economic Times"*

2007 *"Simplicity, Generosity, & Joy"*

These themes helped capture the imagination of our congregation and resulted in growth in giving. One of the things that Paul Scott Wilson's book *Imagination of the Heart* helped me most with was in dealing with how image can be a creative way of focusing worship. Wilson talks about the importance of imagination in preaching. He points out that the more we are able to preach in a way that invites people to respond from the heart as well as from the mind, the more change and transformation can take place. He quotes Charles Rice, who says, "Image evokes image, story calls for story, life speaks to life. . . . But all this depends upon the exegete/interpreter/preacher's capacity to live in the symbol, in this case, the very language and image of the text, to dwell in the house which the text provides. That capacity, an act of the imagination, is the essence in forming sermons."[4]

Worship Based on Prayer

When it comes to designing worship and sermons on financial generosity, prayer becomes fundamental. When I feel anxious about financial stewardship, preaching prayer helps my struggle.

Thomas Troeger's prayer continues to help me as I repeat it over and over again:

God, give me the confidence to trust
in the way you have created me,
so that I may use all that I am
to be attentive to what is
and may thereby learn
how to awaken in my listeners
the same compassion and justice
which was in Christ Jesus. Amen.[5]

Most preachers do struggle with stewardship worship and sermon planning, especially when worship is designed to invoke giving.

Ernest Hunt, in his book *Sermon Struggles*, talks about four methods of sermon and worship preparation that I also found helpful for stewardship preaching. He talks about four methods of sermon preparation that can be used. I would suggest that these four methods of understanding are essential for worship planning. He talks about that which comes from the text, the cultural source, the pastoral situation, and the conflict. I appreciate the suggestion that different perspectives are necessary. How do we catch the image and then decide which method can best help me focus on that image, not only in worship preparation, but also in preaching?[6]

Ernest Hunt continues, "In any case, I have learned that it is the conflict in me, and not necessarily the conflict in writing a sermon, which influences people, while remembering that varying methods as a discipline is a good and healthy habit."[7] He confesses that from his own study of preaching, it is the struggle of the soul, expressed in a methodological way, which causes increased response to preaching.

I agree with Hunt that there are many methods but one way. The preacher must be true to oneself! And he states that that way is to be able to authentically communicate our internal conflict of faith more freely with the hearers. Worship liturgy and prayer can reflect our struggle with money and faith.

Worship Planning Observations

From the 2007 through the 2015 stewardship operating campaigns, we have specifically demonstrated the need for financially focused sermons and worship services to help people with the stewardship of money. Our attendance and giving grew through these stewardship campaigns. In some cases one could observe greater spiritual commitment, contentment, simplicity, and joy in our congregation. Over twenty-five hundred members and visitors took financial classes that brought hope and help to those with a desire to become better stewards of their financial resources.

Leading worship and preaching on financial generosity can often bring challenging responses from some people. Many pastors have been the subject of criticism. Comments are made that can be hurtful, and leadership can be tested. Dr. Kent Keith offers encouragement:

> People are illogical, unreasonable and self-centered. Love them anyway.
> If you do good, people will accuse you of selfish, ulterior motives. Do good anyway.
> The good you do today will be forgotten tomorrow. Do good anyway.
> Give the world the best you have and you will get kicked in the teeth. Give the world the best you have anyway.[8]

Planning worship takes courage, conviction, and assurance that your efforts bring spiritual growth. Renowned author Henri Nouwen says, "Every time I take a step in the direction of generosity, I know that I am moving from fear to love."[9] Designing worship services and sermons on generosity can be an opportunity to help the hearers move from the fear of scarcity to God's love of abundance. Nouwen goes on to say: "Fundraising is a very rich and beautiful activity. It is a confident, joyful and hope-filled expression of ministry. In ministry to each other, each from the riches that he or she possesses, we work together for the full coming of God's kingdom."[10]

As people of all ages encounter God in worship, they experience the joy of giving and grow in faith! Every new generation is presented with different challenges. New worship and communication styles are needed. Generational differences do impact generosity. Worship planning involves people representing different age groups. Involving different age groups in worship is also important. For many older congregations it is imperative to involve younger people. Be creative. Let worship be intergenerational. Lovett Weems suggests that congregations begin slowly and intentionally involve young people. Be sure to provide training and coordination for new worship leaders of all ages.

Creative Planning Advantages

Careful worship planning brings great advantages. In the absence of sensitive, careful planning, a number of difficulties may result. Planning stewardship commitment services requires tender, loving care. Thomas Jeavons and Rebekah Basinger state that over the past fifty years, a chasm has developed in this country between our faith and secular society.[11] They describe different responses that the average Christian may offer when asked to integrate faith and the practice of giving:

1. Indifferent response to the possibility of fund-raising as ministry
2. Reactionary response to refuse to learn how fund-raising is ministry
3. Pious response as a shallow effort to sanctify/make fund-raising a ministry
4. Preferred response to connect fund-raising and ministry that is biblically based

Have we lost the dynamic of doxology in worship today? Too often when we worship we experience the offering as a transaction like taking attendance. Worship planning can offer creative ways to praise God with our offerings so we experience the offering of our gifts to God as transformational and bring glory and praise to God. We need to rediscover the doxology that has disappeared from our worship.

Obviously, we want to plan and execute worship that integrates giving as our faithful response. The preferred result of a worship service is for participants to deepen their faith and spiritual understanding so they will grow in faith as witnessed by the practice of giving. As the psalmist said, "But I have sure faith that I will experience the Lord's goodness in the land of the living!" (Ps 27:13).

Online Resources

Eight Sermon Series Ideas (2007–2014)

Section III

Six Giving Models to Propel Generosity

The purpose of this section is to identify several proven stewardship models for ministry that can inspire, innovate, ignite, and improve generosity in your church or faith-based community. Many stewardship models today are outdated and may lead to a decline in giving. Campaigns that are executed poorly or are not relevant are counterproductive. We all have ministry areas that can be improved, and updating our essential stewardship models is critical. Too many pastors look for the latest popular stewardship campaign model and just plug it in thinking it will provide the necessary funding. The generous church will offer well-planned campaigns that are based on the spiritual and financial needs of your community. Such campaigns propel generosity for Christ and the church.

The challenge of this section is to encourage stewardship leaders who want to learn practical and applicable ways that grow the joy of giving. Growth happens when you develop stewardship models that raise levels of expectation for the pastor, staff, leaders, members, and visitors. Your stewardship models will need to fit your particular community of faith. These stewardship models can become supportive of your faith community's discipleship journey.

Local churches cannot function well without financial stewardship models that support the annual giving; strategic mission and emergency giving; capital/building giving; memorial giving; planned giving; and major donor development. This section will describe these six models and how they can help your community become more faithful and fruitful. I will describe strategic ways to improve these six models in your local church. These models are essential for the church's comprehensive stewardship and generosity year-round ministry.

Before you read the next six chapters ask yourself these key questions:

1. How can I **inspire** vision to raise giving expectations?
2. How can I **innovate** new ministry models that fit my congregation's needs?

3. How can I **ignite** leadership change?
4. How can I **improve** stewardship and generosity ministry to all levels of givers?

It is both a privilege and challenge to serve in Christian leadership today. There are areas of ministry that bring joy and those we try to avoid because they are outside our comfort zone. Today, the challenge of stewardship preaching and leadership is more important than ever before. Financial uncertainty, the aging of the church, and declining attendance are just a few reasons why this challenge feels overwhelming. I know I am in good company—two-thirds of the pastors who consult with me voice this concern.

Peter Senge offers this leadership insight: "Nothing is more limiting to a group than the inability to talk about the truth."[1] Lovett Weems, in his book *Focus*, speaks to the truth of why we need to reset our stewardship models of ministry. He calls for a financial reset of ministry in our church that may require reducing the financial baseline to one that is more realistic.[2] While I know this is true on some levels, I am proposing another way for the local church.

I agree with Dr. Weems that the practice of depending on fewer people to provide more money is unsustainable with the reality of our declining membership in the United Methodist Church. However, I would suggest another way. By resetting our focus on donor development, we may not necessarily have to automatically reduce our budget. There are a number of stewardship models that can be improved. Let's look at the first stewardship model of ministry: the annual giving campaign and how it supports the vision and purpose of the church.

Chapter 7

Annual Giving Campaign

Adam Hamilton has a standard approach to Resurrection's annual stewardship campaign planning that has proven effective. We begin each stewardship sermon series by celebrating what God has done in the past year. It is a time to cast a vision for where God is leading us in the next year. Adam bases his sermons on a biblical approach to tithing, stewardship, and generosity. Each campaign seeks to be relevant to the needs of our members. He begins by asking me and others, "What financial issues and problems do our members need help with this year?" We want to know the felt need of our community.

In 2007, we recognized that many in our congregation were struggling financially—not because we were not making enough money but because we were living beyond our means. National economists were pointing out that people were not saving money. The stock market had not yet crashed nor had the economic recession started, but the signs were alarming to us.

Our stewardship and worship planning led us to design a shift in campaign focus. Adam realized he needed to help people redefine their relationship with money. He asked our people to think carefully and biblically about where we find real joy and what our lives are really about. In other words we reset our stewardship approach. Our annual stewardship campaigns are not based not on what the church wants *from* our members, but on what the church wants *for* our members. We continue to use this teaching approach as we plan every stewardship campaign.

What We Want for Our Members

What does the church want for our members? We want our members to experience financial peace and commitment through good stewardship practices. We want our members to witness that they are growing in their spiritual commitment. We want them to have a heart for giving that blesses them with the joy of generosity. We want them to understand their need to give. We want this understanding to be theologically informed. We want our members to be guided by biblical teaching. We want our members to be blessed as they strive to put God first. We want our members to trust the Lord's abundance and grace in good times and bad. We want all this and more for our members!

Annual Strategic Goals in Giving

Preparing a good stewardship sermon series takes strategic planning. A three-year approach to planning can bring sustained results. When you know your congregation's current giving levels, you can then set measurable growth goals. These growth goals can empower better stewardship and generosity each year through consistent preaching and teaching. For example, measure the percentage of members who return a commitment card each year. Also, measure the average household giving each year to see if there is growth.

The 2007 sermon series was titled *Enough: Discovering Joy through Simplicity and Generosity*. The emphasis was not about increasing our budget but about helping people experience the life God wants them to live. We came up with tools and stewardship teaching models to help people budget, reduce debt, and find greater joy.[1]

Whereas most years we saw a decline in attendance during the stewardship sermon series, this year our attendance increased during the series. As a result, our membership gave even more financial resources the next year while in the face of economic uncertainty. Each year we design our stewardship messages with the specific needs of our congregation and community in mind; and we celebrate growth. Our annual giving to the operating fund has doubled in the last ten years. Our planning each year builds on the strengths of the previous year's campaign. Every year we teach our members that they are giving not to a budget but to God.

Giving to God

I recently attended a conference where the speaker said, "The most important thing about you is what you think about God." He explained this theological statement over and over and in many different ways. He even went on to say, "What you think about God will determine your future." Making God a priority in our living and giving is an essential stewardship indicator.

As a pastor for over forty years, I can tell many stories and lift up much scripture that supports this point. What we think and what we do can be transformative if we understand and experience the truth about God. This is foundational to our theology of giving to God.

So what is the truth about God's expectations when it comes to giving? And if we can discover and act on this truth about giving to God, what difference can it make? How can giving to God bring renewal to the world and to the church? How can giving to God reach new people and new communities to bring help and hope? How can giving to God help each of us live a radical Christian life following the teaching of Jesus and resulting in changing lives? All these questions are vitally important for each of us. They are critical to our church. They are eternal for God's kingdom.

The truth about giving to God is that it is not based in fear. Giving is a practice of faith. Giving helps us. God does not need our money, even though giving is an act of worship that God desires. Giving to God helps us in reaffirming God's goodness, in expressing gratitude, and in demonstrating our faith. Giving to God brings us closer to God like any practice of spiritual discipline and faith expression. Giving deepens our soul and disciplines our self-centeredness.

The truth about God as taught through scripture, tradition, reason, and experience is that God is a generous God. For God so loved the world... God gave his only son. God gave so that we would know something of the Lord's amazing grace and generosity. We give because God gave and continues to give. We give back what God first gave us.

So what you think about God is vitally important for the rest of your life. What you do about God will determine your future. And what you do with your life can either bring glory to God or not. Giving to God as a transformative act of gratitude becomes an act of worship.

Advance Planning

Every year we begin planning for the fall campaign six months in advance. As the executive pastor of stewardship and generosity, it is my responsibility to develop and manage the activity schedule. We review and update the planning schedule based on lessons learned from the previous year, and the upcoming preaching schedule of our senior pastor. Adam designs a three- or four-week annual stewardship sermon series scheduled for October or November.

The planning spreadsheet includes the following:

- Target dates
- Activity
- Those involved
- Owner responsible for the activity
- Completion dates
- Evaluation notes

The schedule calls for planning different meetings for the stewardship team; the senior pastor and worship design team; campaign key leaders; staff and volunteers; the communications team; and the IT team. Since we now have four campus locations, we also meet early in the planning process with the campus pastors. We streamline our planning meetings. We know that our annual stewardship campaign planning is a vital priority that impacts our ministry and mission. I meet one-on-one with the key leaders to execute our plan on schedule.

Communication

Every campaign needs a compelling annual theme that supports the vision and purpose of the church. This theme will often be the title of the sermon series or complement the series in some creative way. The theme appears on the print media, website, posters, coffee cups, video promotion, letterheads, envelopes, and other materials. The theme is uplifting, exciting, and challenging!

Our communications staff also uses social media in timely and creative ways to promote awareness and involvement. Every department of our church encourages support so that we grow the culture of generosity each year. Non-members are not asked to return a commitment card, but members are expected to do so. We do not ask inactive members to return a commitment card, but rather encourage them to become more involved.

Information Technology

Our IT department provides reports necessary for our mailings, e-mail messaging, and other target level stewardship communication. They also help us measure our giving amounts and the percentage levels of member participation. For example, our goal is to have 70 percent of our active members return an annual commitment card. Some years we have had a greater percentage of response. Over the last five years we have averaged 66 percent participation.

Because we have the support of our information technology team, we can target giving and activity levels of our membership. Don Joiner, in his book *Creating a Climate for Giving*, offers a proven argument for multilevel communications. Each level receives a message that best speaks to their giving. People have different levels of spiritual, discipleship, stewardship, and mission-growth needs and interests. Each level is encouraged to step up in their giving.[2] Our IT department helps us track the involvement and giving levels of our members and visitors. For more information on "Segmented Giving Levels for Multi-Level Communication," see Online Resources.

All members need to know what a difference their giving makes and how their giving is an act of faithful worship to God. Everyone needs to be aware that the church knows and appreciates their level of giving. Each level receives a different letter or e-mail to inform, inspire, and invite. We want every member to grow in their giving potential. The larger the church, the more important it is to have excellent information on member activity.

New Members Give Generously

The majority of our new members are non- or nominal Christians who have not been practicing tithing or percentage giving with the tithe as a goal. The money issue may have been a major obstacle to joining. We see many people enjoying the ministries and facilities, but they do not want to make a financial commitment. They know that there are member expectations and one of them is that every member will return an annual commitment card. We want our members to practice percentage giving with the 10 percent tithe being the annual giving goal. We know that if our new members give they can feel ownership responsibility at whatever giving level is possible. So we encourage new members to start somewhere and strive to increase their giving each year.

People who get plugged into the church will financially support our ministries. I send a personal thank-you letter when our records indicate we have received a first-time gift. Saying thank you really encourages new members and visitors to feel welcomed and needed.

A new member giving guide brochure along with a new member commitment card is part of the new member information packet distributed at the Coffee with the Pastor. The senior pastor, Adam Hamilton, shares his tithing testimony and reviews our giving expectations. The executive pastor of generosity and stewardship team members are introduced and are available to greet new members. New members who are ready to return a commitment card do so at the stewardship information table. Those who are not ready to return a card can mail it in the envelope provided or place it in the worship offering plate the next time they are in worship

Invite and Inform Visitors

Monitoring where visitors are in the giving process is also very important. When we know where people are in the giving levels, we can better know how to help encourage giving. Start measuring people in the lower continuum, and find ways to connect with them. Tailor your message to encourage them to start giving. We want to cultivate a stewardship and generosity community. Our message is what the church wants for you, not from you. Giving is more about the need of the giver to give than the recipient to receive when the givers know they are valued.

We talk about people discovering the joy of generosity through simplicity. Adam Hamilton's book *Enough* has helped thousands of pastors and churches with this revolutionary and biblical truth. There is a very helpful *Enough Stewardship Program Guide* that describes every aspect of creating the culture of generosity and joy in your local church. Living simply and with contentment helps us limit our greed and overspending, and encourages debt elimination.

Since the Great Recession this interest in helping visitors and members with financial planning has been very intentional. Our preaching and teaching stewardship also helps people reset their priorities. People are encouraged to get out of debt, save more, and give generously.

A financial coaching ministry helps people eliminate debt and set up a budget. All of us want financial security in an uncertain financial world. That sense of security is built upon biblical principles of stewardship. At Resurrection new members are encouraged to take other stewardship classes along with study programs like Alpha and Disciple Bible Study. Our teaching ministry supports our preaching and our preaching supports our teaching.

We know we can help new visitors by helping them discover where they are going with their spiritual and financial lifestyle. The church can help new Christians grow with incremental steps. We can move them forward in living and giving for Christ and the church as we preach and teach the good news that really helps people. When someone has been helped by the gospel, they in turn want to help others.

Group Life and Congregational Study

There are a number of helpful four- to six-week studies and devotional guides available to promote growth in discipleship and stewardship before or during the stewardship campaign. Ongoing and special classes can be offered to encourage personal and spiritual growth. There are online studies that individuals or families can do in their home or office. Many of these studies are video-based. A daily online study guide called "G.P.S." (Grow, Pray, Study) will also include personal testimonies on the joy of giving.

Small groups help members grow in discipleship, involvement, and deeper commitment to Christ and the church. Involvement in small groups most often indicates much greater giving. (See "Small Group Ministry Is Essential for Building a Culture of Generosity," in Online Resources.) We know that the greater number of people involved in small groups and classes results in a greater giving and loyalty. Financial giving becomes one way our members can grow in their discipleship journey of knowing, loving, and serving God.

Results

Let's return to the key questions when planning the annual stewardship program. Did we cast a vision that raised expectations? Did we develop new and innovative ideas to meet the needs of our people? Did we grow the giving levels so that we experience a greater joy that benefits the purpose of our church?

We know that a good stewardship campaign each year will empower great generosity. Scripture puts it this way:

> And serve each other according to the gift each person has received, as good managers of God's diverse gifts. Whoever speaks should do so as those who speak God's word. Whoever serves should do so from the strength that God furnishes. Do this so that in everything God may be honored through Jesus Christ. To him be honor and power forever and always. Amen. (1 Pet 4:10-11)

Measures That Improve Generosity

Annual stewardship campaigns are much more effective in congregations that emphasize stewardship as a priority, and a call to be deeply committed. In congregations with generous levels of financial contributions, programs that promote estimates of giving annually result in increased giving. Stewardship literature indicates that those who make annual estimates of giving usually give 20–30 percent more than those who do not. Most churches find this to be true and continue to do annual stewardship campaigns. When people plan what they give to the church we also see them doing a much better job of using their own annual budget. When better stewardship happens, greater generosity results!

Here are ten observations that can be documented:

1. In congregations that teach members at different levels of their spiritual journey to grow in their discipleship and stewardship commitment, the results are healthier spiritual maturity and financial health.
2. In congregations where members are connected to small groups, classes, mission projects, and other volunteer and service programs, there is increased giving of time and finances.
3. In congregations where people are informed and excited about what the church is doing year round, there is increased generosity and joy.
4. In congregations that practice annual commitment programs, people will give much more than what they identify on their commitment card when informed and inspired about ministry and mission needs.
5. In congregations that celebrate what God is doing weekly in worship, people will give not just to budgets but also to specific ministry and mission that changes lives for Christ.
6. In congregations where leadership targets communications to different people according to their commitment levels, growth results. Different people hear the same information differently.
7. In congregations that have the expectation of tithing and proportional giving, there are giving goals that can demonstrate growth in discipleship.
8. In congregations that support year-round biblically based generosity, stewardship, and financial management studies, growth in giving results because of deeper discipleship.
9. In congregations where the pastors and leaders set the example, there is generous giving and joyful living.
10. In congregations that conduct annual campaigns, growth in giving will also be observed in special, capital, mission, and planned giving.

Evaluation Is Necessary

At the completion of the annual stewardship campaign an in-house evaluation is completed. This involves a meeting or a survey with all the stewardship team and staff involved. We simply ask the following questions:

1. What went well?
2. What do we need to improve?
3. What new ideas do you have for next year?

Pastors and congregational leaders can study their annual giving and discover helpful trends. For example, identify those who pledged one year but have not pledged for the new year. Every year our stewardship team contacts the non-responders and asks them to complete an anonymous Valued Member Survey. (See Online Resources.) This is done three to four months after the operating campaign and becomes another way to evaluate our stewardship campaign

This survey seeks feedback. It lets our members know that we are aware they did not return a commitment card. They can tell us why by answering these brief questions. Over the years this research has been very informative and helpful in evaluating our ministry. We always ask our pastors to review this list so they can offer care and concern where needed.

How can we maximize gains and lessen the losses in our annual giving? The pastor and key leaders who can be trusted with confidential information need to know who gives what and how that may change each year.

One pastor who is savvy says that every year she looks at giving patterns. She makes personal calls to say thank you to substantial new givers and those who have increased their giving. She also asks them for the story behind their generosity. These stories can then be celebrated appropriately. Generous donors encourage other donors.

Attention is also given to those who have significantly lowered or stopped their regular giving. We know this pattern may indicate a need for pastoral care. Good stewardship results when we nurture relationships with our donors at all levels of giving.

In this chapter we have stressed that our annual stewardship campaigns are focused on the needs of our worshipping community. Our theology of giving is God focused, not budget focused. The practices of advanced planning, good communication, and providing financial giving reports are essential. Attention is given to new members and visitors as we strive to develop new donors.

The reader is also encouraged to review the suggested measures to improve the generosity with your faith community. Evaluate your annual stewardship campaign efforts and find ways to improve each year.

Online Resources

Segmented Giving Levels for Multi-Level Communication

Small Group Ministry Is Essential for Building a Culture of Generosity

Valued Member Survey to Non-Responders

Chapter 8

Strategic Mission and Emergency Relief Giving

People give when they know the need. This is especially true in natural disaster response!

During most of my twenty-five years of being the lead pastor, I did not do effective strategic planning for mission giving. The three churches I served responded when we had a natural disaster, when there was a special denominational appeal, or some local mission needs was made known. Our approach was reactive not proactive; and while our churches always responded well when they knew of a human need, we could always have done better. We did not prepare in advance and we did not always take the time to celebrate generosity in worship on the weekend following the offerings. I have learned in recent years that it is very important to be prepared. Develop a plan that can be implemented almost immediately so that the congregation can know how and when to respond with their gifts.

At Resurrection we started a Christmas Eve special offering for children in poverty in 2007. Every year since then we start strategic planning for annual mission appeals in September. We set our mission giving priorities for the next year. Early approval helps our promotion planning. We plan all events and offerings so that our priorities are clear and we do not overwhelm our congregation with other special requests. We support the general church special offerings through our mission and operating budget rather than making these six additional denominational appeals. We also support conference appeals, advance specials, and other world service needs on a case-by-case basis. We do not want our congregation to have donor fatigue around too many mission appeals in worship. In some cases, we may reach out to and ask donors who have a special interest to give to these mission needs.

Here are Resurrection's six annual mission fund-raising programs:

- Christmas Eve (local and international)—100 percent of the offering goes to mission. Visitors will gladly give to children in poverty, and when visitors give they are more likely to return.

- Golf Classic and Auction (spring)—seminary student scholarships and grants

- Sacred Steps 5K Run/Walk (fall)—Africa health, education, care, AIDS

- Monthly Communion Offering—member and non-member assistance

- Easter Mission Offering—a portion of the Easter offering is given to a local mission organization via a grant competition

- Emergency Offerings—immediate response to natural disasters; mission teams provide hands-on service

Advance planning has allowed us to increase the generosity impact of our church. The Christmas Eve offering in 2012 and 2013 both totaled over $1.2 million. The impact on our community and world for children in poverty continues to grow. Our mission staff and volunteers are leading in ways that are changing lives and transforming communities! Our disaster response teams are organized and trained because of planning and preparation.

We are very intentional in promoting our Christmas Eve mission offering. Many churches may send a special mailing appeal to all members in December. The needs are identified and members are asked to bring their Christmas Eve offering to worship. This traditional Christmas Eve offering may be mission focused. Other churches give to meet their year-end World Service apportionments or other conference benevolences. Churches that are financially solid at year's end may direct their total Christmas Eve offering to second-mile causes. Our visitors find joy in giving when they know 100 percent of the Christmas Eve offering goes to children in poverty. When our visitors give to these special mission appeals we find that they are more inclined to continue visiting and get involved, especially in mission projects.

Your plan could include a mailing or online appeal. In addition, this appeal would be presented via bulletin/e-mail/web announcements and by invitation of the pastor. When we started our Christmas Eve appeal a special Christmas Eve offering envelope would be attached to a bulletin insert in the Christmas Eve bulletin. Our loose plate offering would also be directed to the mission giving. There would be one offering at each service. Prior to the offering a brief video would be used to celebrate our local and global outreach efforts and appeal for generous giving. The musical offertory for each service would focus on the joy of giving.

The offering envelope can be inserted into a bulletin. This envelope would also allow more space to picture and describe the mission benefactors. A Christmas Prayer for the recipients can be printed on the insert. After three years of using envelopes, we no longer do so. Members and guests are assured that all the offering not designed for the operating fund goes to mission for children in poverty.

Suggested scripts and articles would be prepared for our pastors and worship leaders to provide consistency in messaging at our four campus locations. The scripts would also be prepared for the weekend prior to Christmas Eve worship to help prepare our congregation and to promote this mission giving. The theme of this appeal calls for everyone to give a gift equal to the amount spent on another family member.

We have discovered an emerging trend—particularly among high-capacity donors—is away from traditional charitable giving to more strategic mission giving. The goal of strategic givers is to achieve social change by addressing some of the more complex economic and social challenges that foster poverty and social inequality.

What does this trend portend for faith-based organizations and religious congregations? Three guidelines surface as imperative practices for faith communities hoping to attract strategic givers:

- Be accountable and fiscally transparent; these traits build donor trust.
- Inform your donor with a mission statement clearly identifying your program's purpose and strategy; clarity and knowledge nurture generosity.
- Tell stories that reflect your human impact; real-life examples speak to a donor's aspirations and demonstrate your mission effectiveness.

At Resurrection we have found that both growth in giving to the operating budget and strategic mission giving is possible when there is advance planning, communication, and a real commitment to changing lives and transforming our communities. Our members give generously when they know the need. Like many nonprofits and other church agencies, we work to provide a credible process so that all gifts will be used to meet the needs of relief and restoration.

In the face of bad news of natural disasters, the church must be ready to respond responsibly. There are so many nonprofit organizations like the Salvation Army, Red Cross, and others in your local community that are most effective in marketing and immediately asking for gifts. How can the church offer relief and recovery funding?

The church can be there first with relief. But the church can also sustain the people in need with ministries that restore and develop communities. The church can also be the last to leave. Your mission ministry can really benefit by generous offerings from your congregation if you are prepared. If you are not prepared in advance, your response level will be limited and donors may lose confidence in your capacity to handle this need. Do you have guidelines for handling emergencies in a timely way? Staff teams can work quickly to promote emergency giving by using approved guidelines. (See "Finance Department Emergency Disaster Guidelines," in the Online Resources.)

Generosity begets generosity. Do not hesitate to give yourself to the needs of others in crisis. I have seen churches that have effective emergency giving programs grow that actually bring increased giving to operating and other financial needs. Just as we see more and more people serving in mission opportunities, there is a growing trend that mission gifts bring greater loyalty to the total needs of our church.

Online Resources

Finance Department Emergency Disaster Guidelines

Chapter 9

Capital Giving Campaign

Effective capital campaigns result in growing committed discipleship, effective leadership, and greater generosity of the pastor, leaders, and congregation. It is a major project that becomes a top priority for the whole church. The key is involvement with as many people as possible in leadership roles. Many campaigns may involve over 120 leaders serving on up to fifteen teams. However, every capital campaign is different and can be designed to meet the specific goals.

The role of the pastor is crucial for success. The pastor drives the exploration and feasibility to determine if and when a capital stewardship campaign is to be scheduled. A feasibility study may be necessary. The pastor will consider the church's need for a professional consultant. In most cases an outside professional consultant will add value and improve the overall benefits of leadership and generosity for the church.

The pastor is the spiritual and administrative leader of the capital campaign. The consultant is there to coach and assist you. You will guide the selection of key leaders who should also be faithful givers who have the trust and respect of your congregation. Time and prayerful thought must be taken in the selection of your key volunteer leaders.

The consultant will serve as a facilitator and trainer for all meetings. He or she gives direction for the schedule and each phase. Job descriptions and expectations will be provided by the consultant and need to be adapted to fit your particular campaign. One size does not fit all. Make sure that your campaign is organized to fit your congregation's needs. In recent years we have also learned that great attention and development is needed for major donor giving. (See chapter 12.)

It is important to remember that the congregation needs to understand your urgency and confidence in the project. Since this is a challenging opportunity, it may feel overwhelming to you and your church leaders. Be assured that as you plan your work and work your plan the results will be rewarding. The consultant will reassure you that similar campaign models have helped hundreds of churches. While each church will develop its own models, utilizing the key components with committed leaders will result in spiritual and financial growth.

Active and assertive leadership by the pastor and other key staff and leaders is critical as your members want to sense your confidence. Recognize that intensive campaigns can grow the faith and finances in new and dynamic ways. I have observed amazing spiritual growth of the whole congregation during capital campaigns as people learn to give sacrificially Success was made possible by outstanding staff dedication and leadership. The leadership set the pace that involved hundreds of others. Great involvement in the campaign created an amazing energy for everyone. Donors at all levels of giving were truly motivated to give sacrificially and to the glory of God.

Remember to spend personal time with your consultant so that you both can support each other and work together well. The consultant should be someone who fits well personally and theologically with your congregation. The consultant can serve as a personal coach to the pastor and key leaders. Your consultant can help you broaden your perspective and vision for the future and narrow your leadership tasks and focus.

Be sure to personally introduce your consultant to church leaders, staff, and campaign teams. Help build understanding and urgency. Work with the consultant and key staff to write a case statement that is clear, compelling, and concise. The case statement is a purpose statement that expresses the need, plan, and benefits of the campaign in a creative and rhetorical way. Point out the needs in terms that if you do not reach the campaign goal there will be consequences to the future vitality of the church. The consultant will assist you in this. The case statement demands your best effort as you write and perfect it with each version. (See the sample case statement in the Online Resources.)

As pastor, your knowledge, understanding, and love for your congregation is essential. You will give leadership in creating a campaign theme. You will do the major teaching and preaching, but will want to call upon your consultant for ideas. Your consultant will also call upon you for your insight during the campaign. The consultant will view your situation more objectively so you are aware of the pros and cons of decisions. You and your leadership team will make the campaign decisions. Your consultant will guide and support those decisions.

The pastor will want to make the campaign scheduling decisions a priority. The church calendar will make the campaign a priority. There should be no conflicts or competing schedules that might take away from the campaign. The pastor and staff need to give the campaign priority in their personal and professional schedules. The schedule should be completed at least twelve months in advance. It is imperative that you make personal visits for major donor development. Small group events for major donors are also very effective and beneficial. Make sure your donors are available during this time of the year. Give yourself plenty of time (two to three months) for this activity. Capital campaigns are very demanding on church staff and volunteers. Good advance scheduling reduces stress, limits conflict, and helps build team work with results.

Over the years I have seen many benefits from successful capital campaign: new facilities, new ministry and mission, and growth in attendance. More importantly, those involved have experienced spiritual growth. Pastors can help produce these wonderful results by preparing a foundation for the campaign. The campaign begins with the pastor. You lead by your example. You are the source of the vision, the voice of God's call, and the heart of all that happens.

Effective pastors need to realize that their personal examples of sacrificial financial commitment are benchmarks for others to follow. I remember my anxiety when my first capital campaign consultant asked me to tithe. I told him I was already tithing. He said I was tithing for the operating fund; I needed to also tithe for the building fund. Twenty percent for a young pastor with four children was really sacrificial but essential. I believe in sacrificial giving. As my football coach used to say, "No pain, no gain."

Adam Hamilton leads by example at Resurrection as he is open and honest about his sacrificial giving in capital campaigns. He is vulnerable around his anxiety and concerns. Because he shares his honest struggles, others identify with Adam and, by faith, give sacrificially. Financial leaders are both bold and strong in asking for the gift but also model vulnerability and empathy. Adam has a personal way of expressing God's love and our need to belong to the church, while calling us to be generous, courageous, and faithful. He always gives permission for others to disagree with him. This usually disarms those with disagreements. All that we do is for the sake of others and Christ.

Financial commitment can be built on the biblical theme "not equal gifts but equal sacrifice." We often ask, "What am I willing to give up or do without for the next three years?" Financial commitment should be based on one's spiritual commitment. Pastors can help people discover a process to make spiritual decisions that are based on God's will. Prayer guides can help members through a discernment and decision process. I have observed the excitement of members who discover the joy of giving that will make a difference for the next generation.

The consultant will ask you, the pastor, to share not only the amount of your gift but also how you and your family came to that decision. Your church leaders will follow your example in most cases. Gifts for capital campaigns come from many areas: regular income, income-producing and other assets, postponed purchases, and other in-kind gifts.

The following key components in planning and executing a capital campaign are recommended:

Feasibility—Knowing the need/ability of your congregation is the first step a leader takes. This process calls for prayer, followed by interviews with staff and members. Many pastors will use focus groups. It is also wise to do a three-year financial audit on giving potential.

Vision—A compelling case statement is essential. The pastor carefully prepares and casts a clear, concise plan that will benefit the future of the church.

Leadership—Interview consultants, key campaign leaders, and others who can provide effective leadership for your campaign. Select the best leaders that fit the church's needs.

Support—Know what approval process is necessary to garner support for the campaign. Work with key leaders prior to decision-making meetings to promote the need, plan, and benefits. Be sure to answer the difficult questions early in the process of decision making.

Giving chart—Capital campaign consultants develop this tool as a way to reach your giving goal. This profile is especially needed with major donors. It indicates the number of gifts and amounts needed at three levels.

Design—The campaign can be complicated with all the necessary components. An overall design of the phases clarifies the process.

Calendar—Set the schedule for your campaign at least twelve months in advance. The campaign will have priority and should not have conflicts or competition on the calendar.

Teams—Identify team leaders and members early in the process.

Training—Job descriptions are important tools when you interview key leaders. Most will say yes if they know clear expectations and the schedule. Every team member will need to attend the training meetings.

Communication—Prepare a communication plan for all the ways you can promote your campaign. Print materials, video clips, e-mail, social media, and a mailing schedule are all essential.

Preparation stage—Action planning is vital. Every action needs a schedule for the task to be completed.

Information—Develop materials that explain your campaign schedule and benefits. Research potential major donors in your church and community.

Advance commitment—Major donor visits are the most critical aspects of your campaign.

Leadership group events—Igniting leadership group events is an exciting way for the pastor to cast the vision and describe the plan and benefits of the campaign. This meeting provides for early support for the church's needs.

Pre-campaign—Public announcements are important early so members know that a capital campaign has been approved and scheduled.

Special events—Design special events to promote advance commitments. These events can be dinner or dessert meetings. Small group events for major donors often work best. Larger group events can be held with other leaders, staff, and generous donors.

Worship—Creative worship planning is essential to support the three- to four-week campaign sermon series. Worship is the most important platform for the vision and need as the congregation seeks God's will.

Campaign—Sermon Series—Planning by the pastor is the heart of the campaign. This planning needs to begin six to twelve months in advance. Your worship and campaign leaders need to know the preaching theories or series title early.

Response—Every member should be expected to respond with a commitment card. However, most capital campaigns have a goal of at least 50 percent participation of active members.

Commitment—Receiving pledges and celebrating commitments is a very important act of worship. Use several weekends to promote participation. Consecrate these commitments in worship. Plan a celebration worship experience for the whole congregation.

Follow-up—Contact non-responders after two weekends. Use a mailing with an additional commitment card. Ongoing follow-up can be as needed.

Evaluation—What went well and not so well? Develop a survey tool or interview your key leaders. There is always much to learn.

Celebration—Expressing thanks in worship is critical. The pastor can tell multiple stories of generosity and sacrifice. Testimonies can be powerful! Be sure to celebrate the end of the campaign also!

Quarterly updates—Keep the congregation informed and motivated. Develop a quarterly reminder for the congregation. Report on the number and amount of gifts. Always be encouraging!

New members—Invite new members to give during the three-year campaign. Share with them the vision of the capital campaign. Expect them to participate with a commitment card.

Summary

The overarching goal of a capital campaign is to help everyone understand the critical needs of the church. The vision for the campaign can then help inform and inspire people to know that it is more than raising money. The vision and purpose as described in the case statement must be more important than new buildings or money. Buildings are essential tools for growing ministry, mission, and reaching others for Christ.

The pastor plays a critical role in laying the spiritual foundation, which results in financial response. There are four phases:

I. Prayerful Planning

- Knowing the need and casting the vision
- Feasibility study and focus groups
- Leadership recruitment and development
- Getting the right start—scheduling

II. Igniting Interest and Support

- Preparation—prayer focus
- Major donor events and personal visits with pastor
- Information meetings—discernment aids, Q&A materials
- Special events—advance commitment
- Asking for leadership and major gifts

III. Launch

- Town hall meetings for the congregation
- Creative worship planning
- Worship teaching and preaching
- Response

IV. Follow-Up

- Follow-up of the campaign (short and long term)
- Express appreciation to all that were involved in leadership
- Send quarterly giving statements
- Send a thank-you letter when the donors complete their pledged giving
- Contact those who are not giving and express your concern
- Evaluation and celebration of the results of generosity

A capital stewardship campaign is a dynamic process that will call for leadership. You and your congregation will grow spiritually as you make this journey a priority. The pastor's willingness to be a catalytic leader for others is essential. Your personal relationship and coaching skills will be needed as you guide the key leaders of your campaign. In most churches the following key leaders are needed:

- Advance Commitment Leader(s)
- Campaign Leader(s)
- Information Leader(s)
- Prayer Leader(s)
- Children Leader(s)
- Contact Leader(s)
- Enlistment Leader(s)
- Hospitality Leader(s)
- Response Leader(s)
- Special Event Leader(s)
- Print/E-mail Communication Leader(s)
- Student Activity Leader(s)
- Visual Communication Leader(s)
- Follow-Up Leader(s)

Each key leader will work with the pastor and consultant to recruit his or her leadership team. By recruiting and training these teams, greater support is built. In most cases these teams will be made up of talented, dedicated, and generous members. Their leadership gifts are essential! Recruit your very best leaders to have a successful campaign.

Online Resources

Sample Campaign Case Statement

Chapter 10

Memorial Giving

Your local church finance committee may appoint a memorial committee. Memorial committees can benefit those who want to provide a meaningful way to witness their love and thanksgiving for the life of a loved one. Often words seem like an inadequate way to fully express our sympathy.

A memorial gift given through the church can be a very thoughtful expression of sympathy. These gifts honor not only the deceased but also their family. The family can help direct the gifts to fund special needs of the church with the guidance of the memorial committee. In many cases these gifts become lasting memorials or provide for ministry and mission in our community and world.

The following suggested twelve guidelines approved by the memorial committee of Church of the Resurrection may be of help:

Guidelines

(1) All memorial gifts will be deposited and acknowledged by the finance and accounting departments upon receipt with written acknowledgment to the donor as well as to the family of the one in whose memory it is given.

(2) The office of the finance and accounting department will record all gifts including the name(s) of the donor and the person in whose memory it was given.

(3) Memorial gifts will be used at the earliest feasible time. The memorial gifts shall be classified as either:

a) Designated Funds—gifts designated by the family for application to an ongoing church project, special project, program, ministry, or mission. If the fund is over two hundred dollars, a member of the memorial committee will communicate and counsel families as to their wishes and church needs. Funds must be designated within the first twelve months unless the memorial committee lengthens the time frame for designation.

b) Undesignated funds—all other memorial gifts that have not been designated by family/donors.

(4) The memorial committee approves the use of all funds. Any member can request the finance committee to review the decision. Any funds that impact the building facility or land will need final approval by the board of trustees.

(5) Designated or undesignated memorial funds may be transferred to the other ministry areas upon the approval of the memorial committee.

(6) The memorial committee will develop an active list of needs in the local church that are not funded in the church budget and would be suitable for a memorial gift. A copy of the approved list will then be available from the memorial committee. Items suitable for memorial gifts may include, but not be limited to, items of a durable nature that:

a) enhance the worship of God

b) enhance the spiritual growth of the church

c) enhance the fellowship of the church

d) provide a visible support to a ministry of the church

e) support church and denominational mission projects

f) promote the mandates of the Great Commission and our church vision (Matt 28:19-20)

(7) The board of trustees and church staff may submit requests for use of memorial funds. Any such requests should be on a memorial request form and be complete including proper authorizations. A sample request form can be found in the Online Resources.

(8) A memorial book will be maintained by the memorial committee and will recognize designated memorials, being located in a place for congregational viewing. We are developing a new program to provide a memorial touch screen for use by friends and family of the deceased. This touch screen will have the deceased's name, brief description of his or her church involvement, and the benefactor of their memorial gifts. The touch screen will be located in a small chapel or other suitable location. This meaningful memorial information can be easily updated and also available online.

(9) The memorial committee will promote the existence of a memorial program, and prior to or on each memorial weekend will publish how memorial gifts have been used in the previous year.

(10) The memorial committee will review the memorial financial statement at each meeting. An annual financial report will be presented to the finance committee each year.

(11) The memorial committee may consist of six members and will meet on at least a quarterly basis. Three members present at a meeting will constitute a quorum. Members of the memorial committee will be appointed by the finance committee on an annual basis and can serve for a maximum of two three-year terms. The memorial committee will have a chair, vice chair, and secretary. Each year the finance committee will appoint a representative from its committee (one of the six members) to serve on the memorial committee. The director of finance and accounting and the executive pastor of stewardship will also serve with voice but without vote.

(12) It is recommended that the memorial committee give a brief written report to the congregation in worship on memorial weekend. Memorial gifts honor those who have passed away during the last year and enhance the church's ministry and mission. Giving appreciation for memorial giving in worship results in greater giving.

These guidelines have been adapted to meet the changing needs of our congregation. As congregations age the work of the memorial committee becomes more important to the church's generosity ministry. Older congregations have a long tradition of memorial giving and can provide greater insights and experience. It should be noted that many other churches may have more fully developed guidelines and memorial giving programs. Memorial committees are encouraged to update and improve their ministry every year. For example, our memorial committee is now planning to add a touch screen memorial center where family members can find memorial information about their loved ones for years to come. Memorial giving models have meaningful ways of bridging the past and present to the future!

Online Resource

Funding Request to the Memorial Committee

Chapter 11

Planned Legacy Giving

Today, more than ever, people are talking about legacy giving. Marketing and advertising firms are using the word *legacy* to sell products. We know that seven out of ten Americans make gifts to charity in their lifetime but only one out of one hundred may think of leaving a legacy gift to their local church. I believe the main reason for this is that church leaders simply don't ask our members to consider making a legacy gift. After all, our loyal members have given faithfully over many years. They appreciate the opportunity to consider a legacy gift. Just ask members to consider making a legacy gift to the church and discover their interest.

Call to Action

My pastoral ministry had a turning point in the first local church I served. One of our dear saints of the church passed away. Gertie was in her golden years at the time of her death. She had one daughter who was also an active member of our church. After we celebrated Gertie's wonderful life of love and faith, the choir was asked to help her daughter with Gertie's estate sale. Everyone joined in the project and we made a wonderful day of it. We had lots of help and there was great food and fellowship.

When the sale was over Gertie's daughter thanked me for helping and asked me to thank the volunteers from the choir. Then she said something unexpected: "My mom's estate proceeds are going to a church-related college and out-of-state orphanage!" I smiled and said, "Gertie was always generous!" Then I asked, "Why did she decide to send her legacy gifts to these two institutions? Had she ever visited them?"

"No," her daughter replied, "they just asked her by phone and sent her information in the mail." Needless to say, I could not help but celebrate Gertie's generosity to these worthy charities, but over the next few days, it began to dawn on me that I could have asked Gertie to consider a gift to her home church. Our music minister could have asked Gertie to remember the church she loved and supported for decades for a legacy gift. Gertie loved music and our choir. Our music minister said, "I know she would have been very happy to offer a legacy gift for music needs. We just did not ask!"

In my first ten years of ministry I had never asked anyone to consider an estate gift, or spoken about legacy giving. I did not understand that churches could easily set up endowment programs. Local churches can easily partner with area UMC foundations to manage planned gifts that would support the present and future needs of the church.

Since then, I have given pastoral leadership in setting up and expanding endowment programs in three local churches. When I started my ministry at Resurrection, the foundation was three years old. Our senior pastor, Adam Hamilton, had a vision for a legacy program at Resurrection. He saw the vital importance of planned giving to sustain the church's future. Adam's vision for legacy giving is now bearing much fruit. In the last eight years of our planned giving ministry we have grown from thirty to five hundred legacy gifts that represent well over $40 million in anticipated gifts to sustain and grow our ministry, facilities, and mission outreach needs.

This model of generosity is vital to the future of our church. Churches may have an endowment program, but it is often underdeveloped and lacks consistent leadership. Many pastor friends and colleagues report that their church has a small endowment committee. It is there to help if anyone wants to leave a bequest. Otherwise, it is inactive. This type of planned giving ministry model will not bring future growth or vitality! Let's look at these key questions about planned giving:

- Why planned giving?
- What is planned giving?
- When do you know you need a planned giving model?
- How can planned giving be a vital part of your local church now and in the future?

Why Planned Giving?

I will always remember visiting Resurrection for the first time. Adam Hamilton had invited my wife, Lori, and me to consider a new ministry position as executive pastor of stewardship and foundation development director. During that visit I learned from the pastors, staff, and lay leaders why planned giving was so important at Resurrection. The potential for a planned giving ministry had great appeal for me. I was excited to be a part of growing a planned giving ministry that would sustain the future of the church for decades to come!

The Church of the Resurrection was experiencing dynamic growth. God was changing lives, transforming the community, and bringing renewal through this vital church. It was very important to sustain Resurrection's ministry and mission for future generations. But I also learned another reason.

Planned giving opportunities were vital to meeting the needs of Resurrection members. More and more members were realizing that God was calling them to be generous in their annual, capital, and special giving; and God was also calling them to plan for legacy giving. Leaders at Resurrection now wanted a way to start giving legacy gifts.

One of the couples I met had a strong urgency for planned giving. They had a passion for new leadership needed for the church's foundation. I could feel their sense of excitement. Two years later this family gave a major insurance gift to our foundation. This transformational gift will provide funding for future ministry, local mission, and facility needs. Here is their story:

Doug and Nan Smith Testimony

The year was 1985. Doug and I had just been married a few weeks when we decided to become a part of Metropolitan Avenue United Methodist Church. We didn't have a church home, so we decided to attend my husband's grandparents' church. As I reflect on those early years of our marriage, I can see Jesus laying a *foundation* for Doug and me to eventually become a part of the *foundation* at the Church of the Resurrection.

Metropolitan Avenue United Methodist Church was a wonderful place full of well-seasoned Christians who had many life experiences and lots of sage advice to share with a couple of newlyweds! Doug jumped right in and got involved by joining the board of trustees. I worked in the children's programs and tried to help where I was needed. The months and years went by, and we began to see some changes. The people we had grown to love were getting on in years and so was the building in which we worshipped. The building, as beautiful as it was, began to need more that just some paint and a nail or two. There were big-ticket items to contend with such as air conditioning and a new roof. We tried to do some fund-raising, but with many in our congregation on a fixed income these efforts were not very successful. I remember sitting in worship one Sunday watching the water drip from the ceiling into buckets!

In 1990, we began looking for a new church. The change was necessary because we were expecting our first child and wanted a strong children's program for our new baby. About that time, we received an invitation to join a new church meeting in a funeral home! Fast-forward many years to the Church of the Resurrection of today.

As the years have passed, God has certainly blessed Doug and me with many wonderful and life-changing gifts. After much prayer and discernment, along with our past experiences in Metropolitan Avenue UMC, we were led to become a part of the Resurrection Foundation. Currently our church is filled with young, vibrant, wage-earning families. Our building is well-built and seems as though it will be never be run down. However, that same thing could have been said about Metropolitan Avenue UMC fifty years ago!

The Church of the Resurrection has been our church home for twenty-two of our twenty-seven years of marriage. God has worked in our lives in mighty, powerful, and unexpected ways through the people and ministries at Resurrection. I cannot begin to express the love that God has shown us here. We are inspired to help others experience the same. One way we have found to do that is by being involved in the Resurrection Foundation. Through our gifts to the Foundation, as well as our annual and capital campaign giving, Doug and I can do our part to see that Resurrection will stay a vibrant and growing instrument for God's work long after we are Home.

Why does your church need a planned giving ministry? Simply put—for two reasons. First, to sustain your future ministry and mission; and second, to help a growing number of members who feel called by God to leave a legacy gift. Resurrection now has over five hundred members who plan on leaving a legacy gift. The wealth transfer from the boomer generation will be the greatest in human history! Some estimate that for the church the wealth transfer could be over $6 trillion by 2052.[1] To grow in the future, planned giving ministry is essential now.

What Is Planned Giving?

Planned giving in the church can be as simple as asking people to leave a bequest in their will to your church. Planned giving has become so popular today that nonprofit organizations, universities, hospitals, foundations, and charities receive an estimated $17 billion each year. Most annual conferences in the United Methodist Church have foundations to serve the local churches in their area with planned giving help. These area foundations have excellent staff ready to help every local church.

Planned giving should become part of every local church's stewardship ministry, regardless of the church size, age, budget, expertise, or giving history. Your area UMC Foundation can provide information and planning to help you establish an endowment committee.

Members can offer planned gifts in several ways:

1. Deferred gifts (at the time of death)
2. Current outright gifts
3. Expectant gifts that are pledged
4. A combination of gifts

Planned gifts can provide immediate benefit, deferred benefits, or a combination of both. Members who plan on giving a bequest normally will be strong givers to your annual budget needs. They are loyal donors!

Planned gifts can be outright gifts **of stock**, **real estate**, **personal property**, or **cash**. Appreciated stock represents the most common type of non-cash gift. **IRA distribution gifts** are becoming more popular and also represent a considerable tax savings to those over the age of seventy and a half. These are typical planned gifts for the church. The donor's attorney or financial advisor offers the necessary legal advice.

Churches also benefit greatly from **bequest giving**. Bequests are the most popular of all planned gifts because they are easy to understand and do not require donors to part with their assets during their lifetime. This offers donors a sense of financial security and peace of mind knowing that their assets are available to meet some unforeseen expense.

At the church I serve, we encourage bequest giving because it is easy to explain, requires less cost to promote, and once established, is rarely changed. We also recommend percentage giving rather than a specific dollar amount. This way donors do not have to worry about using up the estate if they live a longer-than-expected life. Whether the estate is a small or large amount, the church receives a percentage. Most members consider leaving at least a tithe (10 percent) gift, and the remainder goes to family and other charities. If there is no family or other significant charity, many donors will give the church a much higher percentage.

A **bequest** is simply a written statement in a donor's will or trust directing that specific assets or a percentage of the estate is to be given. The church should encourage members of all economic levels to consider bequest giving.

When deciding on which type of assets to give, donors usually choose the most highly appreciated assets in order to save on capital gains taxes. In this way donors can give more because they have less tax liability. The donor can give the appreciated assets directly to the church. The church then sells these assets and the capital gains tax is avoided thanks to the church's tax exempt status.

Some donors prefer to give through a **charitable lead trust**. It is one of the most sophisticated of all planned giving instruments. It is advisable that an experienced charitable estate planner assist the donor and the church. This charitable lead trust pays an annual income to the church for a certain number of years. The remaining principal goes to the donor or the donor's family when the trust ends.

A **charitable gift annuity** is a simple contract between the donor and the church. The donor makes an irrevocable transfer of cash or property. The church endowment committee or foundation agrees to pay a fixed amount of money each year for the lifetime of one or two individuals. This type of gift is easy to explain and requires minimal administrative time and expense. The guaranteed stream of income provides financial security for the donor. The church receives the balance at the time of the donor's death. The church and donors can request that local bank trust officers or financial investment advisors manage this process.

A **charitable remainder trust** is a trust in which the donor transfers cash or property to a church and in return the donor or others named by the donor receive income from the trust for life or no more than twenty years. When the trust terminates, the balance goes to the church or nonprofit.

There are two types of charitable remainder trusts: the **charitable remainder annuity trust** and the **unitrust**. These trusts are similar, yet they do have a few differences. The main difference is based on how the annual income is paid. Another difference is that the annuity trusts do not allow for additional contributions, while the unitrust does. Most charities and churches prefer not to serve as trustee because of the legal fiduciary requirements and reporting. Churches can use area UMC Foundations or bank or trust companies to manage their investments.

The **donor advised fund** is a new tool for planned giving that many find useful. Rather than setting up a family foundation, the donor can place funds with the existing church foundation or endowment and offer advice on how these funds can benefit the future ministry and mission of the church.

When Does the Church Know That a Legacy Giving Program Is Needed?

The local church, like thousands of other nonprofit organizations, will want to have a way to respond to this growing opportunity of planned giving. Even with budget limitations, churches can promote the basic planned giving opportunities to receive bequests. Faithful members who have been donors all their life want to give. Their loyalty makes it likely that they will remember the church in their will, if asked.

How Can Planned Giving Become a Vital Part of Your Church?

For churches that want to create an endowment program, it is important to first write a purpose statement. Establishing an endowment committee will then create a strategic plan that outlines goals and objectives for the next three years. The mission and purpose statement is clear and compelling and is approved by the church council.

A concise description of the purpose of the endowment program is then promoted. The potential donors will know that their gifts will serve the future needs of the church. Potential donors will be interested in the financial stability and growth potential of the church. The financial staff will provide reports on investment performance. The church will honor the donor's wishes for the use of the gift.

It is important to know that people will give generously if they know the need. People give when they have trusting relationships with the pastor and leaders. At Resurrection, our members direct giving and planned gifts to our Seminary Student Scholarship Endowments and Funds. We know the expensive cost of seminary education. We know that most pastors start their ministry with educational debt. People give to causes, and seminary scholarships are vitally important to our future pastoral leadership.

Before introducing an endowment or planned giving program, you may want to invite a staff member from your area UMC Foundation who can articulate the merits of planned giving to your church board. If you have an existing program you may want to use a consultant to revitalize your efforts.

Leadership Principles

Relationships are especially important for a church's financial growth. Perhaps the most important task of a church foundation board or endowment committee is effective partnerships between the pastors, staff, and elected leaders. Committees and boards that consistently make their decisions based on the church's mission are most effective.

Annual strategic planning helps set measurable goals. These goals are based on real needs that will shape the giving and generosity each year. Creative thinking happens before the goals and objectives are finalized. Research data and analysis supports the ministry and mission planning.

Transparency and any conflict of interest need to be addressed openly. Leaders may sign an annual conflict of interest policy. In this way there is clear compliance with integrity among church leaders.

Annual reports are prepared by church leaders. The annual all-church meeting celebrates the ways in which ministry and mission have made a difference. Gratitude is expressed for the congregation's generous giving. Appreciation sustains the vitality of leadership.

Transparent expectations of boards and committees need to be written and taught each year. Job descriptions that are clear produce results. Every board of leadership team should revitalize themselves by term limits, leadership development, teaching, and devotional times at each meeting; and they should always express gratitude for the giving of God's people and the blessings of God.

It is also important that leadership represent the diversity of the congregation in age, gender, and membership tenure. Dynamic leadership can bring new ideas and opportunity for change.

Most importantly, leadership measures the results and celebrates changed lives. At Resurrection, we seek to fulfill our vision of changed lives, transformed communities, and renewal of churches. This is leadership with a vision!

Preparing for Future Needs

Legacy giving is possible for every church member, not just the wealthiest. With the growing number of people in the boomer generation, the potential is enormous.

Christ-centered members who give regularly and generously to the church over their lifetime will want to consider a legacy gift. What we ask is simply, "Would you consider a tithe (10 percent) of your estate as a legacy gift to the church? Legacy gifts are a wonderful witness of faith and love to your family, friends, and especially our church family!"

Planned giving is an investment in the future of our church's purpose to change lives for Christ and reach out to our community and world in mission. Most donors want to give an endowed gift that will be invested, and the gain on that investment income will provide ongoing ministry. Some members may direct their legacy gifts to be used in the first few years as the needs arise. This type of gift goes to an investment fund that can be used as the need is evident; however, most legacy gifts go to endowments. Endowment funds invest the gift and then may use the annual investment return for ministry needs.

With the closing of so many mainline churches every year, a critical question needs to be asked: What kind of future church will we have? Endowed or extinct? Churches with endowments have greater financial security and health.

Legacy gifts are given in many different ways: will or trust, insurance policy beneficiary designation, gift transfers from an IRA, life income (annuity) gift, and other types of endowment gifts. This can be done as easily as designating the church as a beneficiary on a life insurance policy, bank account, or pension account; or with the help of an attorney, a more sophisticated instrument like a charitable trust can be established to benefit the church.

It may not occur to even faithful members who have given throughout their lifetime to the Lord's work to leave a legacy gift to their local church. Our boomer generation is the largest in US history to be transferring wealth over the next thirty years. Now is the church's opportunity to ask, to teach and preach, and to celebrate legacy giving.

Churches need diversified revenue streams of income to achieve consistent, mission-based outcomes. Legacy and endowment gifts provide a lifeline to the future by enabling churches to achieve long-term financial stability and sustainability. In many cases, endowments can support the facility needs, scholarships, and other special needs that otherwise might become a burden to a church's budget.

Legacy gifts offer a powerful means to enhance and diversify a church's funding efforts because:

1. Almost all members are potential legacy donors in the local church because they have demonstrated their loyalty with ongoing giving and involvement.
2. In most cases, the largest gift most people make is a legacy gift.
3. Legacy programs do not add a burden to the church's budget. However, a pastor or staff member does need to give oversight to a program that may involve a number of volunteers.

4. Legacy donors make larger annual gifts than non-legacy donors.
5. Only a small percentage of members have been asked to make a legacy gift, so there is greater potential. In the church I serve, we put the legacy gift option on the annual commitment card.
6. In most every area or annual conference there is a United Methodist Foundation to help you set up your legacy giving program and assist you in asset management and leadership training.
7. There are a wide variety of legacy gifts, many of which are easy to create.
8. Legacy gifts are one of the few sources of giving that can increase during tough economic times.
9. There will be a staggering transfer of wealth over the next fifty years. The church can ask its members to consider a legacy gift to sustain the future of its ministry, mission, and facilities.
10. Most local churches have members who can and will offer their professional service to help set up or support an endowment program.

Develop Your Plan

Most churches do not have an active legacy giving program. I have consulted with churches that have set up an endowment program, but in many cases it has been inactive. It has been very passive in its appeal and has been forgotten by the majority of members. While this is a leadership problem, it usually happens because the pastoral leadership and endowment committee have not developed annual goals and plans.

First you plan your work. Then you work your plan! Development plans make all the difference as they set up annual goals and strategic objectives to achieve those measurable goals. Constant communication to the congregation is essential. Our first plan called for an annual weekend celebration and promotion of planned giving in our worship services. (See Online Resource, "Resurrection Foundation Development Three-Year Plan.")

Basic Components of Your Development Plan

If the following list looks like a lot of work, it is! But once it is completed with annual goals and strategy, it only needs to be updated.

1. The Purpose of This Plan—to reach future generations for Christ
2. Challenges and Opportunities (SWOT: Strengths, Weaknesses, Opportunities, Threats)
3. Benefits of the Development Plan/Changed Lives
4. Annual Strategic Objectives

- Strategy for each objective
- Target audience
- Specific responsibilities/roles
    - Development committee
    - Donor relations committee
    - Investment committee
    - Executive pastor
    - Staff and volunteers
- Annual activity schedule
- Personal contact
    - Follow-up by board members to information requests
    - Donor development plan by executive pastor
        - Self-declared donor/record keeping
        - Prospective donor
    - Visits by executive pastor
    - Advocates and directors

5. Long-term Strategic Goals and Objectives (three years)
6. Long-term Target Audience
    - Segmentation of donor levels for communication
    - Marketing age levels
    - Membership tenure targets
7. Communication Tools
    - Web page
    - Written and electronic
    - Bulletin and e-note
    - Social media
    - Year-end giving brochure
8. Annual Timeline for Events and Activities
9. Annual Evaluation, Report, Recognition, and Celebration

Benefits of Your Development Plan

Reaching future generations for Christ and the church is the ultimate goal of this planning. It is important to set annual goals and plan ways to achieve success. You can anticipate that your planning will:

- Improve performance
- Stimulate forward thinking
- Clarify future direction
- Solve organizational and financial problems
- Survive, even flourish, with confidence
- Build teamwork and expertise
- Influence rather than be influenced
- Meet immediate and future financial needs without burdening the annual budget

In the United Methodist Church, every area has a United Methodist serving the local church. We also have a nationally focused local church United Methodist Foundation. Your area UMC Foundation is there to help you establish or revitalize your legacy program. These foundations have excellent leaders and have been serving our churches for decades.

Self-Assessment Ideas

You might want to simply begin by asking questions. We ask these types of questions of our church leaders every few years. Interview five to ten active leaders and members and staff of your church with questions like these tailored to your specific situation:

1. From your perspective, what is the purpose of a foundation or an endowment committee?
2. What do you see as the relationship between legacy giving and annual stewardship giving?
3. What are the **strengths** of your legacy program?
4. What are the **weaknesses** of your legacy program?

5. What **opportunities** do you see for your legacy program?
6. What are the **threats** to the future of your legacy program?

We used a set of questions designed to:

- Gain insight into the level of awareness, knowledge, and understanding of your legacy giving program.
- Find out what your program is doing well and how it could improve.
- Explore actions to avoid and those to pursue.
- Identify ways to increase church members' commitment to making the endowment committee or church foundation a part of their financial legacy.

Share information about the current state of your legacy giving program.

Being Donor Focused

Helping donors discover the ways that their gift has meaning is the most important part of stewardship ministry in a local church or faith-based organization. The driving force behind giving is a person's spiritual purpose. Planned giving makes spirituality real and establishes a lasting legacy of faith and love. We are here to serve the donor!

How can we create a caring resonance as you visit with donors? Donors find great satisfaction in helping sustain the areas of ministry that they want to advance. Ask yourself in what ways your conversation can be more fulfilling spiritually for you and your donors. I often structure my visits around what needs are identified by the donor. I then help the donor's dreams match the needs of the church. Conversation continues around the specific plan and benefits of the particular planned gift.

Donor Motivation

Donor motivation can be clarified in these personal conversations by actively listening. Follow-up correspondence and visits can also restate the purpose of the gift and the donor's motivation. Here are some obvious motivations that cause the donor to give:

- Trust and confidence in leadership
- Excellence in ministry and mission

- Christian values being preserved
- Changing lives for Christ
- Making a difference through mission
- Loyalty
- Joy and personal satisfaction
- Financial stability of the church

Kennon L. Callahan, in an analysis for faith-based organizations, discusses five "motivational resources" to "advance the motivations for giving in yourself and your congregation":[2]

1. Compassion: "sharing, caring, giving, loving, serving, supporting"
2. Community: "good fun, good times, fellowship, affiliation, belonging, a sense of family and home"
3. Challenge: "accomplishment, attainment, achievement"
4. Reasonability: "data, analysis, logic, and thinking that 'it makes good sense'"
5. Commitment: "dedication, faithfulness, duty, obligation, vows, loyalty"

The Wall Street Journal reported on a small college in Kentucky that received a $250 million gift. Tiny Centre College in rural Danville, Kentucky, received stock from the A. Eugene Brockman Charitable Trust. The trust was created in 1981 by the donor who had attended the college and later served on the school's board for a few years.[3]

Someone helped Mr. Brockman develop a planned gift over thirty years ago that is now going to transform this college and the students it serves. It recently announced that forty full-ride scholarships will be available each year for those outstanding students studying science and economics. Many problems can be created by large gifts like this if your church is not prepared in advance. Undue conflict may result.

While we do not know the inside story of this amazing planned gift, we can state that A. Eugene Brockman had an extraordinary sense of loyalty to his college. He was blessed with great financial resources and knew the importance of long-range gift planning. He has made a difference for Centre College, and it in turn now has the resources to impact the lives of hundreds of college students who will change the world!

Planned Giving Process

Planned giving is the process by which good stewards make great generosity happen. Jesus taught several powerful parables about the vital importance of stewardship as an expression of being a faithful disciple of Christ. The biblical and theological process of stewardship can be described as follows:

1. Receives God's gifts gratefully
2. Tends them in a responsible and accountable manner
3. Shares them in justice and love with others
4. Returns them with increase to the Lord[4]

This model of stewardship comes from the Roman Catholic perspective and reflects their tradition and biblical interpretation. The question for each church or faith-based organization is: What clear and compelling stewardship and generosity model will guide what we do and how we do it? This model becomes a teaching tool that serves everyone. It will guide the preacher in the pulpit, the planned giving practitioner, and the person in the pew.

Planned giving can be a unique stewardship model. While Wesley's stewardship model of making all you can, saving all you can, and giving all you can still has impact for today, Wesley finished well. He planned to give away all that he had for the Lord's work. We need a focused planned giving stewardship and generosity model that informs, instructs, and inspires.

Planned giving also helps the donor identify a number of end-of-life faith issues that other stewardship models may lack. For example, how does our faith help us better prepare for living longer, incapacity, extraordinary health care measures and death? Planned giving helps us faithfully finish well.

Bob Buford is a well-known author who has written a number of helpful books for those preparing for retirement and significance in the second half of life. Buford talks a lot about "finishing well." He identifies the growing interest that people have in leaving a legacy of faith and love. His resources and those of the Halftime Institute have been very helpful to the development of our Crossroads ministry for the baby boomer generation. At the United Methodist Church of the Resurrection, we have started a new ministry called Crossroads: Navigating the Second Half of Your Life. For example, for the last three years we have offered pre-retirement seminars. There is great interest in financial management and planned giving in the second half of life.

An Inheritance of Faith

In the closing of the first book of the Bible (Gen 49) Jacob left a legacy of faith and love to his family: "'Gather around so that I can tell you what will happen to you in the coming days.'...He blessed them by giving each man his own particular blessing" (Gen 49:1, 28b).

A planned giving stewardship model will expand the biblical and theological model mentioned earlier. It can be based on these six faith principles:

1. We trust that God is the source of all gifts.
2. We gratefully receive and celebrate these gifts.
3. We provide good stewardship and management.
4. We practice generosity in a life that witnesses justice, compassion, and care for others.
5. We live within our means and multiply resources.
6. We leave a legacy to the glory of God and for the benefit of others.

For United Methodists this legacy model can be supported by scripture, tradition of the church, reason, and experience as guided by the example of Christ and empowered by the Holy Spirit. Our generation has been blessed by the generosity of previous generations. Our task then is to continue this legacy for those who follow us.

J. Richard Ely, who served as executive director of planned giving and stewardship for the archdiocese of Boston until his death in 2011, introduced the concept of "Later Life Planning" to enhance the more secular and traditional planned giving models. It involves three stages that occur in our second half of life. These three realities of (1) ability to live a fully active life; (2) incapacity; and (3) death call for comprehensive planning. Traditionally, this means good planning includes a will and/or a trust, a durable power of attorney, and a health care directive.

Richard Ely suggested that people of faith also consider an "ethical will" in their estate planning. This ethical document can include instructions for living a life with moral values and clear expectations. It can include generational stories to be passed on as a legacy gift. Mr. Ely recommended a particular website designed to help others with financial and ethical planned giving (http://www.ethicalwill.com).

This website resource suggests some common legacy themes not always found in standard wills:

1. Importance of personal values and beliefs
2. Vitality of spiritual qualities
3. Hopes and blessings for future generations
4. Lessons learned in life
5. Expressions of personal and spiritual love
6. Importance of forgiving and being forgiven

The church and faith-based organizations can help prepare for life but often fall short in giving end-of-life direction. The end-of-life dilemma grows greater as more people live longer lives. How can we best address planned giving into the end of life needs? Pastoral care and teaching on grief, finding meaning in suffering, aging, health care decisions, and finding spiritual significance are all vital to our life's journey.

At a National Conference on Planned Giving,[5] J. Richard Ely presented practical suggestions on how the church and nonprofits can better serve others and increase planned giving benefits. I will adapt and update these as follows:

1. Make sure planned giving becomes part of your ministry and that it has a budget that can promote programs like estate planning workshops.
2. Make planned giving part of your discipleship and stewardship teaching and preaching.
3. Know your faith tradition's values and practices that support legacy giving as an act of faith. Lift up memorial giving as part of leaving a legacy.
4. Put a face on all the different needs and opportunities of giving. Provide estate planning events for all people.
5. Include prayer, scripture study, and mission outreach in the planned giving process as it relates to the purpose and vision of the church.
6. Engage the leadership of boards and ministry teams in legacy giving opportunities.
7. Don't forget God in your life. How is God calling you to serve in a way that future generations will be blessed?

Establishing a purpose for planned giving can involve every area of the church's ministry. Marketing and promotion of legacy giving can demonstrate how these gifts can enhance our ministry to children, youth, and adults. Planned giving can be an opportunity more than an obligation when it is faith based and future directed.

Online Resources

Resurrection Foundation Development Three-Year Plan

Donor Profile for Legacy Giving

Estate Planning Seminars

Estate Planning Seminars for Women

The Legacy Journey

Chapter 12

Major Donor Development

What is major donor development? It really is all about developing relationships. The church, from the very beginning, was about building relationships that led to becoming a community of believers in Jesus Christ. George Barna states, "In that context, it is alluring to conceive of fund-raising as a relational activity in which the donor gives out of a sense of loyalty and devotion to the church."[1]

In most cases loyalty will result in people's generosity. Even if building relationships in the church does not result in giving, we are called to build relationships in order to build up the body of Christ, the church. Our task is to reach all members to give generously. Pastors can learn how to make every visit an opportunity to include expressing appreciation and encouraging generosity.

The Pastor's Role

For some time church leaders have observed that 80 percent of the money comes from 20 percent of the givers. Obviously, it would be healthier if there was a better balance in giving. The danger is that a few major donors might gain influence or power and some may want to hold the church hostage. An antidote to this problem might be to raise money from a broader base of people. I believe the best way to do this is to grow the number of donors and, especially, major donors. What would it look like if 40 percent of the members (the major donors) gave 80 percent of the money in most local churches and 60 percent of the members gave the remaining 20 percent? As the church membership grows older it is critical to increase the number of major donors at different age levels in each local church.

Since the 2008 Great Recession some churches report that the ratios are changing. Now, many pastors report to me that 90 percent of the giving may come from 10 percent of the members. This trend is very problematic. It is also true that too many pastors do not know the donor's level or patterns of giving. If asked, most pastors would not be able to name the major donors. Some pastors do not have access to the giving records of their members and have no way of measuring giving levels.

Clif Christopher addressed this dilemma more boldly than anyone I know. He states, "If pastors choose not to know how their members are doing in financial stewardship, I believe they are committing clergy malpractice. They are denying themselves a tool that could help diagnose a person's spiritual condition and that should be what pastors are all about."[2]

He goes on to confront this financial giving leadership problem. "In summary, I can find no good reason for a pastor not to know (what people give) other than to keep the sinners from grumbling."[3] Clif Christopher defines major giving ministry as simply having the right leader ask the right person to be asked at the right time for the right amount.

In order to have a fruitful conversation with a donor, there are a number of key preparation steps that must be completed.

Step One—Prepare a Giving Level Segmentation Chart

Churches that use segmentation programs to track the levels of giving can invite and encourage growth in giving at all levels. More and more donors can step up to higher levels of giving. The purpose of effective segmentation stewardship programs is to increase loyalty, performance of giving, and a greater commitment to biblical stewardship principles. An effective segmentation strategy will help develop more members who become major donors.

Pastors can set up a segmentation chart by first benchmarking levels of giving. For example, the following sample chart would be a good way to start.

Giving Levels	Number of Giving Units
$0	160
$1–$2,000	300
$2,001–$6,000	240
$6,000–$10,000	70
$10,001–$15,000	30
$15,001 and up	10

This chart can be analyzed each year to measure the financial health of giving. Consecration stewardship programs have long used a step-up chart to increase member giving. Both models teach the importance of measuring generosity. All members of the church need a clear expectation to give proportionally with the goal being the tithe.

Most pastors consider major donor development to be a task only when conducting a capital campaign. However, major donor development is essential for annual giving programs as well. It used to be that 80 percent of the donors gave 20 percent of the money, and 20 percent gave 80 percent. Annual giving may now be measured in the following way:

70 percent of the donor base give 20 percent of the money

20 percent upgraded gifts give 20 percent of the money

10 percent major gifts give 60 percent of the money

It would be wise to do a giving audit of your local church. What are your percentages? Measure all giving the last three years. Then set new three-year giving goals. A development plan can then be prepared. Communication plans can also be developed to encourage each group to increase their giving. In my experience this development plan is the best way to create a culture of generosity at all giving levels. Develop an annual plan that communicates appreciation, encouragement, and clear expectations. Avoid the danger of fewer donors giving more dollars by increasing giving at all levels.

Step Two—Know the Reality of Giving Today

When we understand today's reality of American philanthropy, should we be concerned? This is a key question. Dr. Judith Nichols, director of new directions in philanthropy, states that it is not the amount of money that nonprofits raise that matters. What really matters is how much mission and ministry results. She states, for example, "With more than 2,500 registered nonprofits in our Kansas City region vying for less than $16 billion in annual giving, securing contributions remains challenging and competitive."[4] At an Association of Professional Fundraising event on February 20, 2014, Dr. Judith Nichols pointed out the realities of giving are changing dramatically. She makes these four points:

- The overall giving is flat.
- Competition keeps increasing.
- Giving is shifting from "self-oriented" nonprofits to those that are "altruistic."
- Individual giving is decreasing.

All this is to say that to raise more funding for ministry and mission we must better understand the context of what is changing in our community. This understanding will help us develop a more focused plan to communicate our message and reach our donors. Local churches need a comprehensive stewardship and generosity development plan. This yearlong plan includes education to help people better manage money, communication, celebration of generosity, worship, preaching, and other events that inform and inspire giving.

Once this annual plan is developed and executed, local churches can begin to see results. Most plans will take three to five years to see real, measurable results if you want to create a culture of generosity. Improvements can be made each year by evaluating what you do and what resulted. Having a well-thought-out mission-based development plan will help your organization or church develop donors who want to make a difference. The key is to articulate your mission and vision in all that you do. Develop a plan each year to determine who your target audience will be. However, our primary purpose is not in fundraising. Our ultimate purpose is meeting the mission needs of those we serve, to God's glory.

Individual giving is trending down. In 1977, 85 percent of all charitable giving was from individuals. It hit a low of 71 percent in 2007, and has only increased to 73 percent by 2012. Individual giving is the only real source of financial support for most churches. Other sources of funding for nonprofits include foundations, corporations, and bequests. While churches receive bequests, they are few because in most cases church leaders do not ask or encourage estate giving.

Another fact affecting local church giving by the middle class is changing. In 2012, the top 5 percent of earners accounted for almost 40 percent of personal consumption expenditures in 2012. This was up from 27 percent in 1992. Consumption among the top 20 percent grew to more than 60 percent, while the bottom 80 percent dropped to 39 percent. There is a shrinking middle class, which has serious implications for individual giving to the church. There is less discretionary income for more people

The middle-class family has an average annual income of seventy-five thousand dollars. Of that amount, ten thousand dollars is considered discretionary income. There is more and more competition for this discretionary income. For example, everyone, even children, say they "must have" the latest smart phone, tablet, or whatever the newest thing may be.

Another alarming statistic about individual giving points out that by 1990 high inflation rates had caused the average American donor to have half the impact with what his or her charitable gift provided in the 1920s. This long-term view and understanding of inflation is essential for churches and nonprofits if we are to grow our ministry and mission. Even with greater giving our impact can be less and less.

Step Three—Care and Confidentiality

Ethical accountability is essential, especially in any donor communication. It is good stewardship of relationships to practice confidentiality. Perhaps this is all the more reason that the pastor be involved, especially in any personal communication. Any lists of potential or active major donors must be guarded and only available to limited pastors or staff who handle financial records.

In creating a major donor list you can begin to list those who are your top 10 percent givers. This is a simple step, but it would be good to review the last three years of giving records to make sure you are not missing someone.

Creating a list of potential major donors is more challenging. How do you best identify and qualify these donors? The Fundraising School suggests three categories that they describe as Linkage, Involvement, and Advocacy. Nonprofits use this language in the donor development process.

The church could best identify those who have longer membership tenure, or key leaders, or those who we think have the capacity to give. We could call these categories loyalty, leadership, and capacity.

There are many other donor qualities that you will want to consider. Involvement levels, circles of influence, and levels of spiritual maturity are other areas to research when seeking potential donors. Who are your key volunteers? In some situations, even new members may demonstrate a high capacity and commitment level of giving.

The process of major donor development takes time. Trust needs to be built. Pastors could develop a schedule to visit prospective donors.

Nonprofit development staff may make ten contacts and visits each week. A local church pastor could contact and visit at least two potential donors weekly. When a pastor already has developed a good relationship with members, the potential for increased giving is greatly enhanced. This is true for all levels of donors. It is all about relationships.

I recall visiting with one church member four times a year for nearly eleven years. I had a wonderful pastoral relationship. Years later, when the member died, I learned that she left her significant legacy to her church.

Step Four—Making the Money Ask

John Wesley took stewardship of God's money very seriously, as we should. However, we do not live in the 1700s with the Puritan ethic. How do we ask for money in a culture today that avoids talking about giving money? When we prepare to ask for a gift to support our ministry, we want to be well prepared. We also want to make the prospective donor's needs and interests a priority. We want to communicate that the purpose is not what the church wants from its people, but what it wants for its people!

In today's world, making the money ask is a difficult task. This is especially true for most pastors. And yet, financial stewardship is essential for sustaining our vital ministry and mission now and in the future. Since the 2008 Great Recession, the understanding of money has taken on a sense of urgency. Philip Goodchild writes, "Theology cannot be neutral here. As Saint Paul well understood, the central question of theology is that of the essence of the power (1 Corinthians 15:24)."[5] He argues that while we need a science of money we also need a new theology of money. Money has power and purpose that we need to understand in today's economic reality. He identifies four key attributes of money:

1. Money offers a promise and value.
2. Money measures all other values.
3. Money has a speculative value of worth.
4. Money sets up debt or social obligation.

While money is a condition for liberty, power, and prosperity (as Goodchild points out), it is also a condition for generosity. The way we Christians use money also makes it a condition of our witness. Our theology of money begins with our understanding of the very nature of God. God is the supreme model of generosity. As followers of Jesus, we are called to give of ourselves for the benefit of others and as a witness to our creator.

We also trust that our Christian charity will aid the growth of God's kingdom and the proclamation of the good news of Jesus Christ. Christians have long been committed to giving money to help the poor and powerless in our world. We know that we are called to be cheerful givers (2 Cor 9:7).

In the United States today, there is also a greater sense of philanthropy. There are twice as many nonprofit 501c3 organizations than there were a few decades ago competing for the charitable dollar. In the 1980s, 52 percent of charity went to religion. In 2013, that percentage had dropped to 31. The church must ask boldly if we are to sustain our future ministry and mission outreach.

Having been a pastor for over forty years, I believe that God calls us to ask boldly for the gifts necessary for our church's future. It is up to each of us to make it happen with warmth, joy, and generosity for God's people. We believe in an incarnational theology that calls us to follow the example of God. "We love, because God first loved us" and "we give because God first gave to us." This is the message for our affluent and materialistic society for today.

There are at least four dimensions to asking for a major donor gift. We want to review these dimensions as a part of our prayerful preparation. The first is an understanding of the theology of giving. The second is the exploration of the interpersonal psychology and attitudes around asking for money. The third dimension is making the connection with the donor's dreams. We want to know and honor the vision and values of the donor. The fourth dimension is the process that connects the donor and his or her dreams with our specific financial ask that needs his or her support. We also want to be able to deal with any objections or sincerely express our appreciation. If any of these steps is neglected, the results may not be satisfactory. We want our people to experience the joy of generosity.

Theology of Giving

If you are the one requesting the donation, it is vital that you know what you believe. Take some time to think deeply and develop your own theological framework that fits your leadership values and style. Remember that John Wesley built the Wesley Chapel that opened on All Saints' Day, November 1, 1778. Wesley was involved in a number of projects that required major gifts from many supporters.

Here are several Wesley essentials about giving:

1. Wesley taught that giving was a significant part of the very nature of God. God is the source of all good gifts. Life itself is grace. It is free and unearned. As Christ gave of himself sacrificially, we too are to give in his example.
2. Giving is an indispensable witness of our Christian discipleship. Giving is part of our holy living and becomes a spiritual discipline. Our growth in discipleship results in our growth in generosity.
3. Everything we are and have comes from God, our creator. We did not bring it into this world and we cannot take it with us when we die. We trust God in all situations.
4. Giving involves sharing what we have with the poor. Wesley's regular visits and care for the poor is an example for us today.
5. Giving includes offering a voice on behalf of the voiceless. It involves justice and social outreach to support community. As Wesley said, "Money is an excellent gift of God, answering the noblest ends. In the hands of his children it is food for the hungry, drink for the thirsty, raiment for the naked . . . a means of health to the sick, of ease to them that are in pain. It may be as eyes to the blind, as feet to the lame . . ."[6]
6. In Wesley's sermon "The Use of Money" (1744) he said, "Gain all you can, save all you can, and give all you can." Generosity is a spiritual gift for some. These gifted Christians do well when it comes to earning, saving, and giving all they can. They are blessed with the spiritual motivation and personal ability to lead the way in generosity.
7. God expects all those who believe to follow our biblical teaching and traditional practice of giving our time, talent, and treasure to build up the church and transform the world with our witness in Christ.

8. We give because God gives. When we give we can lead by example. We believe that Christians are to serve as Jesus Christ to humanity and represent the incarnated Word of God to all people by our living and giving.

Interpersonal Psychology of Asking for Money

I attended The Fund Raising School sponsored by the Center of Philanthropy at Indiana University.[7] There I was trained in the principles and techniques of fundraising. Here are some of the teaching points that I have adapted for my own use:

1. People love giving and getting. We see this in the joy of giving and receiving gifts. People like to do it for a variety of reasons. It is always helpful to discover why the donor wants to give.
2. Giving money helps us impact our community and serve the needs of others. Giving to meet the needs of the church is also a way to impact our community.
3. Giving is very personal. When making the ask for money, it is very helpful to know the personality type of the donor(s).
4. Some of the main reasons most of us dislike asking others for money are important to understand. They are:
   - We don't want to be rejected.
   - We don't want others to question our motives.
   - We don't want to appear self-serving or greedy.
   - Talking about money seems taboo and too personal.

Attitudes about Asking for Money

The Fund Raising School at the University of Indiana also offers some very insightful points about our cultural attitudes toward money and fund-raising that can be adapted to benefit the work of the church:[8]

1. In the United States, we tend to talk about money only under specific circumstances to a limited number of people. For many people, money is similar to other taboos such as sex and sexuality, death, religion, and politics.
2. It is important to note that many countries and cultures do not have this taboo about money, and that this taboo is not genetic or natural. As

anyone with children knows, children have to be taught not to ask for money. As such, because we learned this taboo, we can unlearn it.

3. This unlearning process requires an examination of the role of money in our society. Think about the meaning of our most common expressions, such as "Money doesn't buy happiness," or "Time is money," or "Neither a borrower nor a lender be." Think of how often one hears the New Testament misquoted, "Money is the root of all evil." (The true quote is "The love of money is the root of all kinds of evil" [1 Tim 6:10.])
4. At the same time that people are taught to believe that money is evil, they also are taught that money has power. Most people believe they would be happier if they had more money, even when presented with story after story of profound unhappiness in the lives of wealthy individuals and families.
5. These very mixed feelings we have about money are projected onto people whom we ask for money, and this further complicates the process of soliciting a gift.
6. It is important to reflect not only on what the culture teaches us about money but also on what we learned in our families. This will be related to the culture, but each family has its own attitudes toward money issues, and some of these attitudes may be detrimental to effective gift solicitation.
7. To be an effective fund-raiser, a person must come to terms with his or her issues about money and must understand the critical role money plays in this society.
8. Once a person has challenged the notion that talking about money is taboo, he or she can move on to challenging the notion that asking for money is rude.
9. Remember that when you ask someone to support your organization, you are asking him or her to invest in work that he or she wants to see happen and cannot provide alone. One person cannot be a symphony, a hospital, or a university. One person cannot clean up the air or prevent illegal dumping of hazardous waste or ensure the civil rights and liberties of women or minorities. People who value any of these things, however, will join with hundreds, thousands, or even millions of other donors in making sure organizations that can do this work exist.
10. When you talk to someone about making a donation to your group, the majority of the conversation is about the good work of your organization, not about money. You then provide the donor with the choice of helping or not helping your group accomplish this work.

Making the Connection and Listening to the Donor

The process of asking comes after you know as much as you can about the donor. You also want your conversation and approach to be built upon your own theology and interpersonal skills. You need to be sincere and authentic.

There are four basic steps when visiting with a potential donor:

1. The **opening** conversation establishes rapport. Talk briefly and in general about the weather, current events, family, or other general subjects and begin to feel comfortable with this person. During the opening you are making it easier for the prospects to shift focus to your ministry and away from what else is on their minds. Listen to their concerns but find a way to make a transition to your focus.

    Suggested Script—(5 minutes)

    1. Acknowledge their role in the church (be sure to research their attendance, giving, length of membership and involvement levels).

    2. Thank them for the opportunity and purpose of the meeting.

    3. Share your commitment and love for the church.

    4. Note that you are not here to ask them for a final answer to a gift today. Ask them to think and pray to seek God's direction.

2. **Engagement.** Bring the subject of the giving goals into the conversation quickly but not rudely. Ask the prospect questions and allow the prospect to ask you questions. Questions can be simply to establish information.

    Listen and respond in ways that honor the donor's interests. Show that you are open to discussing hard questions. A prospect may have observations about the church's finances, board involvement, or leadership of staff or pastors. If you are open to discussion, not defensive, and prepared to share information, the prospect can ask these questions and get some resolution of his or her concerns.

    After discussion back and forth (15 minutes), it is appropriate for you to guide the conversation for a short time with a full description of your program and the money needed to make it happen. Accentuate the positive. Be open to questions.

    Listen for clues to how the donor can get involved and be supportive.

3. **Asking**. This actually started when the prospect gave you permission to visit and ask for a financial gift. All that is left to determine is the amount of the gift and the method by which that gift will be made. Look at the prospect and ask confidently for the gift. Make a specific ask for the donor to consider. Know ahead of time the amount or range amount of your ask. You have a right to be

there. Your church or ministry needs and deserves the financial support. The prospect has told you he or she is open to being asked. They may respond at that time or they may request more time to consider and pray about the amount of the gift.

Suggested Script—(15 minutes)

1. Provide the donor(s) a copy of the Giving Chart that lists the levels of needed giving.

2. Explain the goal. Note that you are asking for a commitment over a two-to-three-year period.

3. Note that there are some who can give on the top tier of the three-tier chart.

4. Share that everyone will be asked to make a sacrificial gift.

5. Explain your own willingness to make a sacrificial gift.

6. Make the ask: "As you look at the gift profile, would you prayerfully consider a top commitment?"

7. Give them time (pause) to respond.

4. **Appreciation.** Offer a closing prayer of thanks or offer a personal blessing. Express appreciation for their consideration of a gift with warm and personal words.

Follow up with a thank-you note or phone call within a few days.

(Total visit should be 40 minutes.)

Conventional wisdom and pastoral sensitivity should be used when seeking the donor's support. Here are the key points to remember:

- Give yourself before asking others to give. Set an example and be willing to share the amount of your gift, if necessary.

- People do not give to causes; they give to people with causes that change lives! Make a case for how these gifts are going to change lives.

- We do not have the right to deprive anyone of the privilege of saying no.

- If your knees are shaking, stomach uneasy, tongue dry just before you are ready to start on a solicitation visit, remember the time-honored admonition: "Kick yourself aside and let your cause walk in." Pray that you can be Christ for this cause.

- The principal reason people do not give: they're not asked.
- Rarely do we know the donor's real interests and often, when we ask, they will tell us what their dreams and visions are.
- The solicitation is never completed until you close.
- Honor the donor by asking at the right level, at the level of the donor's perception of his or her own ability to give.
- Effective solicitation is the right person soliciting the right prospect for the right gift at the right time for the right purpose in the right way.
- Effective solicitation is 60 percent listening and 40 percent talking.

Major Donor Giving is the Hope of our Church

As I look back to my ministry of over forty years I can say that some of my most humbling experiences have been when I have be able to help a donor make a major gift. These transformational gifts changed the lives of the donors, their families, our church, and generations to come. I have seen how the Holy Spirit works with our anxious human nature to open our hearts to giving joy that changes lives for Christ and the church. You can grow generosity as you simply ask donors to consider making a gift. As you practice good stewardship, you will find more and more people will respond in ways that result in great generosity!

Online Resources

Discover Donors in Your Church and Community

Twelve Steps to Receiving Transformational Gifts in the Church

Online Resources

Visit http://www.cokesbury.com/forms/digitalstore.aspx?lvl=free+downloads to download a free PDF of resources for your church. Password: joQB7X7ufh

Additional resources will be posted quarterly at www.claytonlsmith.com. You may contact Rev. Dr. Clayton L. Smith at revclaytonsmith@gmail.com for more information or to inquire about his speaking and coaching availability. Clayton enjoys being of help to you, your church, or nonprofit organization.

Notes

Foreword

1. "Giving USA: Americans Gave $335.17 Billion to Charity in 2013; Total Approaches Pre-Recession Peak," Lilly Family School of Philanthropy News, Indiana University-Purdue University Indianapolis, June 17, 2014, http://www.philanthroly.iupui.edu/news/article/giving-usa-2014.

Preface

1. Donald W. Haynes, "Wesleyan Wisdom: Stewardship, evangelism: antidotes to disturbing trends," *The United Methodist Reporter*, October 15, 2010, http://www.moumethodist.org/console/files/oFiles_Library_XZXLCZ/review101510_JZKR26XR.pdf.

Chapter 1: A Call for Leadership

1. Adam Hamilton, "Change, Innovate, and Improve," (conference, Leadership Institute, Leawood, KS, 2008).

2. Adam Hamilton, *Enough: Discovering Joy Through Simplicity and Generosity* (Nashville: Abingdon Press, 2009).

3. Lovett Weems, *Focus: The Real Challenges That Face The United Methodist Church* (Nashville: Abingdon Press, 2011), 5.

4. Melissa S. Brown, "Giving USA: The Annual Report on Philanthropy," Giving USA Foundation (conference, Kansas City, June 26, 2012).

5. Ibid.

6. Arthur C. Brooks, *Who Really Cares: The Surprising Truth About Compassionate Conservatism* (New York: Basic Books, 2006), 34.

7. Ibid., 7.

8. Warren B. Hrung, "After-Life Consumption and Charitable Giving," *The American Journal of Economics and Sociology* 63, no. 3 (June 24, 2004): 731–745, doi: 10.1111/j.1536 7150.2004.00312.x.

9. Lyle E. Schaller, *The New Context for Ministry: Competing for the Charitable Dollar* (Nashville: Abingdon Press, 2002), 61.

10. Sam Hodges, "UMC in U.S. still shrinking," *The United Methodist Reporter*, March 2, 2012, http://www.moumethodist.org/console/files/oFiles_Library_XZXLCZ/March22012Review_YPCYC7JW.pdf.

11. "Resources: 50+ Fact & Fiction," Immersion Active, http://www.immersionactive.com/resources/50-plus-facts-and-fiction/.

Chapter 2: Casting a Vision for Stewardship and Generosity

1. Robert Schnase, *Practicing Extravagant Generosity: Daily Readings on the Grace of Giving* (Nashville: Abingdon Press, 2011), 11.

2. Randy Alcorn, *Money, Possessions, and Eternity* (Carol Stream, IL: Tyndale House Publishers, 1989), 172.

3. Gordon MacDonald, *Secrets of a Generous Life: Reflections to Awaken the Spirit and Enrich the Soul* (Carol Stream, IL: Tyndale House Publishers, 1989), 21.

4. Ron Blue, *Faith-Based Family Finances: Let Go of Worry and Grow in Confidence* (Carol Stream, IL: Tyndale House Publishers, 2008), 3.

5. Ron Blue, *Generous Living: Finding Contentment Through Giving* (Grand Rapids: Zondervan, 1997), 36, 54.

6. Robert Schnase, *Practicing Extravagant Generosity: Daily Readings on the Grace of Giving* (Nashville: Abingdon Press, 2011), 12.

7. Ibid., 12–13.

8. Gordon MacDonald, *Secrets of a Generous Life: Reflections to Awaken the Spirit and Enrich the Soul* (Carol Stream, IL: Tyndale House Publishers, 1989), vi, vii, xxi.

9. Robert Schnase, *Five Practices of Fruitful Congregations* (Nashville: Abingdon Press, 2010).

10. Joseph Grenny, *Influencer: The New Science of Leading Change*, 2nd ed. (New York: McGraw-Hill, 2013).

11. Vijay Govindarajan and Chris Trimble, *The Other Side of Innovation: Solving the Execution Challenge* (Boston: Harvard Business Review Press, 2010).

12. Walter B. Russell, "God and Giving: The Road to Generosity," in *Revolution in Generosity: Transforming Stewards to be Rich Toward God*, ed. Wesley K. Willmer (Chicago: Moody, 2008), 63.

13. Karl Barth, *Church Dogmatics*, vol. 4, part 1, *The Doctrine of Reconciliation* (Edinburgh: T&T Clark, 1957), 41.

14. Excerpts from a talk to the Marguerite Bourgeoys Family Service Foundation, Montreal, Quebec, Canada, September 16, 1992.

Chapter 3: Creating a Committed Church Community

1. Herb Mather, *Lay Speakers Lead in Stewardship* (Discipleship Resources 1997), 3.

2. Patrick Lencioni, *The Advantage: Why Organizational Health Trumps Everything Else in Business* (San Francisco: Jossey-Bass, 2012).

3. Tim Thompson, "What Is Your Giant?," *Frazer Heart and Home Devotional*, March 22, 2014.

4. Henri J. M. Nouwen, *A Spirituality of Fundraising* (Nashville: Upper Room Books, 2010), 17.

5. John Wesley, "The Use of Money," *The Works of John Wesley*, sermon 50, http://www.umcmission.org/Find-Resources/John-Wesley-Sermons/Sermon-50-The-Use-of-Money.

6. Adam Hamilton, *Enough: Discovering Joy Through Simplicity and Generosity* (Nashville: Abingdon Press, 2009).

7. Adam Hamilton, *Enough: Discovering Joy Through Simplicity and Generosity Stewardship Program Guide* (Nashville: Abingdon Press, 2009).

Section II: Insights for Preaching and Worship

1. Craig A. Loscalzo, *Preaching Sermons that Connect: Effective Communication Through Identification* (Downer's Grove, IL: Intervarsity, 1992), 10.

2. Adam Hamilton, *Unleashing the Word: Preaching with Relevance, Purpose, and Passion* (Nashville: Abingdon Press, 2009).

Chapter 4: Moving Forward—Six Transformational Steps

1. John Calvin, *Institutes of the Christian Religion* (Philadelphia: Westminster, 1960), 1024.

2. Barbara Brown Taylor, *The Preaching Life* (Boston: Cowley, 1993), 76.

3. Fred B. Craddock, *Overhearing the Gospel* (Nashville: Abingdon Press, 1978), 22.

4. Haddon Robinson, "Preaching on Money: When You've Gone to Meddlin," *Preaching*, http://www.preaching.com/resources/articles/11567255.

5. Stephen Hart and David Krueger, "Integrated Faith and Work," *The Christian Century* 109, no. 22 (July 15-22, 1992): 683.

6. Timothy J. Bagwell, *Preaching for Giving: Proclaiming Financial Stewardship with Holy Boldness* (Nashville: Discipleship Resources, 1998), 4.

7. Willard Jabusch, *The Person in the Pulpit: Preaching as Caring* (Nashville: Abingdon Press, 1980), 117.

8. Myron R. Chartier, *Preaching as Communication: An Interpersonal Perspective* (Nashville: Abingdon Press, 1981), 7.

9. Henry Grady Davis, *Design for Preaching* (Minneapolis: Fortress, 1958), 43–44, 126.

10. Fred B. Craddock, *Preaching* (Nashville: Abingdon Press, 1985), 182.

11. Fred B. Craddock, Bible Study Tapes: Parables, Cassette 1, JBC Cassette Service.

12. Fred B. Craddock, *Overhearing the Gospel* (Nashville: Abingdon Press, 1978), 43.

13. Paul L. Holmer, "Kierkegaard and Theology," *Union Seminary Quarterly Review* 12, no. 3 (1957): 26.

14. Fred B. Craddock, *Overhearing the Gospel* (Nashville: Abingdon Press, 1978), 26.

15. Henry Grady Davis, *Design for Preaching* (Minneapolis: Fortress, 1958), 126.

16. Carol Doran and Thomas H. Troeger, *Trouble at the Table: Gathering the Tribes for Worship* (Nashville: Abingdon Press, 1992), 109.

17. Charles Keating, *Who We Are Is How We Pray: Matching Personality and Spirituality* (Mystic, CT: Twenty-Third Publications, 1988), 4.

18. Fred B. Craddock, *Overhearing the Gospel* (Nashville: Abingdon Press, 1978), 83.

19. G. J. Chelune, *Self-Disclosure: Origins, Patterns and Implications of Openness in Interpersonal Relationships* (San Francisco: Jossey-Bass, 1979), 2–3.

20. J. Randall Nichols, *Building the Word: The Dynamics of Communication and Preaching* (New York: Harper and Row, 1981), 127.

21. Joseph Luft, *Of Human Interaction* (Palo Alto, CA: National Press Books, 1969), 135.

22. Abraham H. Maslow, *Motivation and Personality* (New York: Harper and Row, 1970), 41.

23. John R. Claypool, *The Preaching Event* (New York: Harper and Row, 1989), 47.

Chapter 5: Fast-Forward—Seven Insights That Propel Preaching

1. Richard Lischer, ed., *Theories of Preaching* (Durham, NC: Labyrinth, 1987), 80.

2. Hans van der Geest, *Presence in the Pulpit: The Impact of Personality in Preaching* (Atlanta: John Knox, 1981), 144.

3. Clyde Fant, *Preaching for Today* (New York: Harper and Row, 1987), 102.

4. Phillips Brooks, *Lectures on Preaching* (Grand Rapids: Zondervan, 1907), 115–116.

5. Donald F. Chatfield, *Dinner with Jesus and Other Left-handed Story-Sermons: Meeting God through the Imagination* (Grand Rapids: Zondervan, 1988), 5.

6. Fred B. Craddock, *The Gospels*, Interpreting Biblical Texts (Nashville: Abingdon Press, 1981), 47–52.

7. Donald F. Chatfield, *Dinner with Jesus and Other Left-handed Story-Sermons: Meeting God through the Imagination* (Grand Rapids: Zondervan, 1988), 9.

8. Paul Scott Wilson, *Imagination of the Heart: New Understandings in Preaching* (Nashville: Abingdon Press, 1988), 252.

9. Kristine Miller and Scott McKenzie, *Bounty: Ten Ways To Increase Giving At Your Church* (Nashville: Abingdon Press, 2013).

Chapter 6: Creative Worship Planning

1. Eugene Grimm, *Generous People* (Nashville: Abingdon Press, 1992).

2. Adam Hamilton, *Enough: Discovering Joy Through Simplicity and Generosity Stewardship Program Guide* (Nashville: Abingdon Press, 2009), 7.

3. Ian Pitt-Watson, *A Primer for Preachers* (Grand Rapids: Baker Book House, 1986), 69.

4. Paul Scott Wilson, *Imagination of the Heart: New Understandings in Preaching* (Nashville: Abingdon Press, 1988), 21.

5. Thomas H. Troeger, *Imagining the Sermon* (Nashville: Abingdon Press, 1990), 29–30.

6. Ernest Edward Hunt III, *Sermon Struggles: Four Methods of Sermon Preparation* (Greenwich, CT: Seabury, 1982), xvii.

7. Ibid.

8. Kent M. Keith, *Anyway: The Paradoxical Commandments: Finding Personal Meaning in a Crazy World* (Makawao, HI: Inner Ocean Publishing, 2001).

9. Henri J. M. Nouwen, *The Return of the Prodigal Son: A Story of Homecoming* (New York: Doubleday, 1992), 131.

10. Henri J. M. Nouwen, *A Spirituality of Fundraising* (Nashville: Upper Room Books, 2010).

11. Thomas H. Jeavons and Rebekah Burch Basinger, *Growing Givers' Hearts: Treating Fundraising as Ministry* (San Francisco: Jossey-Bass, 2000), 154–7.

Section III: Six Giving Models to Propel Generosity

1. "Exploring Off the Map" (Conference, Leadership Network, May 23–26, 2008 Broomfield, Colorado).

2. Lovett H. Weems Jr., *Focus: The Real Challenges That Face The United Methodist Church* (Nashville: Abingdon Press, 2011), 9.

Chapter 7: Annual Giving Campaign

1. Adam Hamilton, *Enough: Discovering Joy Through Simplicity and Generosity Stewardship Program Guide* (Nashville: Abingdon Press, 2009), 7–8.

2. Donald W. Joiner, *Creating a Climate for Giving* (Nashville: Discipleship Resources, 2002), 70–3.

Chapter 11: Planned Legacy Giving

1. John J. Havens and Paul G. Schervish, "Millionaires and the Millennium: New Estimates of the Forthcoming Wealth Transfer and the Prospects for a Golden Age of Philanthropy," Boston College, October 19, 1999, http://www.wealthtransfernevada.com/pdf/Boston%20College%20Study.pdf.

2. Kennon L. Callahan, *Giving and Stewardship in an Effective Church: A Guide for Every Member* (San Francisco: Jossey-Bass, 1997).

3. Darren Everson, "When Tiny Centre College Was Big," *The Wall Street Journal*, July 31, 2013, http://online.wsj.com/news/articles/SB100014241278873241362045786398819281 06680?mg=reno64-wsj.

4. *Stewardship: A Disciple's Response: A Pastoral Letter on Stewardship*, National Conference of Catholic Bishops (1992).

5. J. Richard Ely Jr., "Planned Giving in Faith-Based Organizations: Making the Spirituality Real," National Conference on Planned Giving (lecture, Grapevine, TX, October 2007).

Chapter 12: Major Donor Development

1. George Barna, *How to Increase Giving in Your Church: A Practical Guide to the Sensitive Task of Raising Money for Your Church or Ministry* (Ventura, CA: Regal Books, 1997), 33.

2. J. Clif Christopher, *Not Your Parents' Offering Plate: A New Vision for Financial Stewardship* (Nashville: Abingdon Press, 2008), 27.

3. Ibid., 50.

4. Judith Nichols, Association of Professional Fundraising Event (lecture, Kansas City, MO, February 20, 2014).

5. Philip Goodchild, *Theology of Money* (Durham, NC: Duke University Press, 2009), 4.

6. John Wesley, "The Use of Money," *The Works of John Wesley*, sermon 50, http://www.umcmission.org/Find-Resources/John-Wesley-Sermons/Sermon-50-The-Use-of-Money.

7. The Fundraising School, Center on Philanthropy at Indiana University, "Principles and Techniques of Fundraising," 7:1–4.

8. Ibid.